From
Self to Self

✻

Notes and Quotes in Response to
Awakening to the Dream

Leo Hartong

NON-DUALITY PRESS

NON-DUALITY PRESS
6 Folkestone Road Salisbury SP2 8JP United Kingdom
www.non-dualitybooks.com

For more information visit:
www.awakeningtothedream.com

ISBN 0-9547792-7-4

From
Self to Self

With gratitude and appreciation to:

Tony Parsons, Nathan Gill, 'Sailor' Bob Adamson
and the many voices of the One.

∽   ∽   ∽

Since things neither exist nor don't exist,
are neither real nor unreal,
are utterly beyond adopting and rejecting,
one might as well burst out laughing.

Longchenpa Rabjampa - Tibet, 14th century

Contents

Introduction

You hold in your hands a compilation of expressions, questions and answers that came about in response to the book 'Awakening to the Dream.' What is being communicated here is something immediate and simple. It is about who or what you truly are right at this instant. Paradoxically it also is a mystery that can appear complex when the mind tries to catch it in a net of words and concepts. Let me say right from the start that such attempts will fail. For that reason this writing does not claim to be an explanation, but it is presented as an exploration through a collection of pointers that rely on repetition and metaphor.

Here is the first metaphor, in which this text is compared to a book about humor. Humor is a great topic. However, we can talk and write about it all we want without ever taking hold of its essence, whereas merely telling a good joke at the right moment IS humor. Of course humor is not limited to telling jokes, and many pages can be filled in an attempt to grasp the ungraspable essence of humor. Such a book can promote laughter, but it cannot tell you how to get a joke. One either gets it or not. When one does not get it, explaining the joke usually kills it. So what to do? Nothing… or perhaps let's just tell some more jokes until one hits home. All this for no special reason, but if I have to give one, it would be that joy shared, is joy multiplied.

So here is a small joke/quote:

Man will occasionally stumble over the truth, but most of the time he will pick himself up and continue on.

~ Winston Churchill ~

The second metaphor, which is used repeatedly in this book, shows that something clear and simple can seem complex when we try to put it into words. The metaphor is space; it is clear and obvious as a direct experience, yet seemingly mysterious when we attempt to describe it. We could for example say that space is nothing, but that nevertheless all objective appearances depend on it. We could say that we see it everywhere, yet we could as easily describe it as invisible. We could say that it has no location, or we could say that it is everywhere and that everything that has a location appears in it. As you see, this description is full of seemingly mutually exclusive observations, which make everything said here true and untrue at the same time.

So, everything appears in space, but where does space appear? It appears on, in – and as an expression of – something even more subtle.

The merest description that can be given to this consciousness is that it is as fine, as subtle, as space. In Maturity your consciousness is God.

~ Nisargadatta Maharaj ~

We can give this subtleness names such as Pure Awareness, Consciousness, Essence, Tao, the Supreme Identity, God, the Self, or simply IT. The word 'IT' may seem to lack warmth, or any other attribute, but it is precisely this lack that makes it such a good pointer. The mind finds it impossible to turn the word 'IT' into a picture, which is perfect, as it points here to the Ultimate Subject, which cannot be made into an object. This Ultimate Subject is the True Identity, 'your' Original Face, or Pure Awareness. IT is what you are, not just what you think you are, and like space IT is simple, clear, obvious and yet indescribable.

Here are some other metaphors to help us point at the indescribable: We can learn to play the piano, but what the experience of music entails, and what musicality actually is, cannot be learned from reading. Also, we may know the taste of a peach, but we cannot tell this to someone who never ate one. Our words can guide the interested person to a fruit seller or a peach tree, but only the tasting itself will answer her question.

This text is pointing you to the metaphorical peach tree of what you truly are, but it does not claim to explain the 'taste' of this essence. Once it is tasted, the pointers have served their purpose. One can then read books like this for the pleasure of reading, or completely forget about them.

ೞ   ೞ   ೞ

The fish trap exists because of the fish; once you've gotten the fish, you can forget the trap.

The rabbit snare exists because of the rabbit; once you've gotten the rabbit, you can forget the snare.

Words exist because of meaning; once you've gotten the meaning, you can forget the words.

Where can I find a man who has forgotten words so I can have a word with him?

~ Chuang Tzu ~

1. God's toothache

Question: Are you saying that knowing all pain and suffering is universal, frees one from it? Doesn't pain and suffering continue to exist whether it is seen as that of the microcosm or the macrocosm? Is it God's toothache?

Answer: At the relative level of the game, life is experienced through the polar opposites such as pleasure/pain, good/ evil, high/low, on/off and so on. These contrasting poles are known from and – generated by – the perspective of an apparent separate character. All apparent free will of this illusory character is aimed at getting away from the minus pole and moving towards the plus or pleasure pole.

The end of suffering is not found in the eradication of one pole while maintaining the other, but suffering's true nature might become clear by asking who it is that suffers.

Liberation can come through the realization that there is in fact no separation anywhere and that there is no individual that does the suffering. In this recognition, fire still burns, the wind still blows, the rain comes down and the sun shines, for all... and for no one.

It is not so much that one is freed from suffering as that it is realized that there is no one to be freed. This perspective is pointed to in the following quote, which has been assigned to the Buddha:

The deed there is, but no doer thereof.
Suffering exists, but no one who suffers.

Suffering is content. Awareness is context. Awareness is the source in which all arises and dissolves. Awareness remains unaffected, just like the mirror remains empty, regardless of what seems to appear in it. Recognize that you are the unaffected Awareness/Witness to which the person and its experiences – good and bad – are a witnessed object. HERE the point of gravity shifts from content to context. This context is empty and marvelous and it does not suffer. It is the peace prior to the mind-generated divisions of good/bad, pain/pleasure, yin/yang. You are that Peace.

ᖇ   ᖇ   ᖇ

You are the unchangeable Awareness in which all activity takes place.

Always rest in peace. You are eternal Being, unbounded and undivided.

Just keep Quiet. All is well. Keep Quiet Here and Now.

You are Happiness, you are Peace, you are Freedom.

Do not entertain any notions that you are in trouble.

Be kind to yourself.

Open to your Heart and simply Be.

~ Papaji ~

2. How to deal with opposing approaches?

Question: Some Advaita teachers say: 'Recognize who you really are, train in that recognition and get stabilized in that recognition'. Others say there is nothing to gain, there is no you; there is just this!

The first approach offers me a method to deal with my emotions, frustrations and my mistaken belief of being a person. Although I appreciate the latter approach, it offers me no method to attain stabilization in That which I really am.

Do you have suggestions how to deal with these opposite approaches?

Answer: Methods for dealing with emotions are fine, but they belong to the realm of psychology and have very little or nothing to do with clear seeing. Such methods are about comforting and adjusting the person. What is discussed here is about seeing through the person as an illusion, not about giving the person methods. The person working on the person is as likely to succeed as a trap that has been set to catch it self.

The problem with trying to get THERE is that it automatically confirms NOT being there. It confirms that there really is a separate you that has to get somewhere later on. This keeps the illusion of separation and time alive and well. There truly is no separate character to reach a future state of timelessness.

This is about the recognition of what it truly is that lives, thinks, sees, and breathes, through and as the apparent character. It is the One Substance. It is as it is, just THIS... Presence Awareness. 'Little you' can't become stabilized in it, but YOU are That.

Response: It's all so fascinating – it's all done with smoke and mirrors! Ashtavakra says 'the world is a magic show' – and so it is. To the topic: the author's reply states that the emotions have little or nothing to do with clear seeing, but does anything have to do with clear seeing? Clearly not. For what is there to see? And who is there to see 'it'??

Our words trip us up in every case. neti, neti, neti. Questions?, maybe, but answers? no.

Dattatreya (the Avadhut Gita) says it's all prattle. But oh how we love our prattle!

Answer: Yes, all our questions, answers and responses are words by their very nature. No one will try to drink the word water, but when it comes to talking about THIS, sometimes it is forgotten that words are mere symbols. As such they point AT, but can never contain THAT, which contains the words. Nevertheless I love the words of Ashtavakra and Dattatreya.

So here are some more words:

What I said was not so much that emotions have nothing to do with what is pointed at, but that methods for working *on* emotions have very little or nothing to do with it. That it equals working on the person instead of seeing through the person.

In the end there is only THIS which cannot be captured in words; It simply is/isn't including apparent characters and emotions. If words make no sense we can always notice the spaces between them, or the background on which they appear.

Response: Well maybe there are answers after all – yours was a good one and I thank you for it. Actually there are and there are not – this is the best of all possible worlds!

I like the idea of seeing 'through' this person that I usually think that I am – actually that I 'always' think that I am when I am thinking. It seems that I can only see through when I stop thinking. STOP THINKING! It's like the space between words or the spaces between inhalation and exhalation. I remain 'the nectar of knowledge', homogenous existence, like the sky.

⁶ᵒ ⁶ᵒ ⁶ᵒ

I AM

'I am the supporter of the universe, the father, the mother, and the grandfather. I am the object of knowledge, the sacred syllable OM, and the Vedas. I am the goal, the supporter, the Lord, the witness, the abode, the refuge, the friend, the origin, the dissolution, the foundation, the substratum, and the immutable seed.'

From: 'The Bhagavad-Gita' translated by Dr. Ramanada Prasad

3. Splitting IT

Question: I have an intuitive sense that fundamental to sustaining the sense of being a separate individual, is the tendency of the mind to split the whole of creation into a 'good' and 'bad' side, where the one is wanted and the other is unwanted.

This split manifests in both overt and subtle ways. Religions manifest the split in a very gross, 'in your face' way. I was at a church wedding the other day, and was treated to a most hilarious manifestation of that split by the priest on duty. I found it highly entertaining, but on another level, it reminded me again of how powerful this belief system is, which splits life into 'good' and 'evil', 'heaven' and 'hell', 'sin' and 'virtue'.

Many people have left this kind of 'gross splitting' behind and have embarked on so-called 'spiritual or psychological paths of self-discovery'. But the split continues. In Jungian circles, they will talk of 'loving your shadows into wholeness'. But... the so-called 'shadow' IS already the wholeness! Other people embark on strategies of 'embracing everything, both pleasant and unpleasant feelings', which is again a more subtle manifestation of the same split, whereby the 'separate individual' still tries to transform the unpleasant to get to a state that is more pleasant. We could continue giving examples: all paths are based on this split, whether it's gross and 'in your face' or more subtle and seemingly refined.

The paradox to me is that even in awakening, this split continues. It is not that we reach some 'ultimate state of pure unconditional love whereby we have no more preferences'. That is just bullshit. The character is part of the play and will therefore continue having likes and dislikes. To put it bluntly: any human being will prefer a walk on a beautiful beach above a dark torture chamber. It's a lot easier to see 'the divine' in the playful innocence of a little child than in a bloodthirsty rapist. So, what actually changes? Yes, I know that source manifests as 'all that is' and that 'all that is' is expressed in duality. There can be no manifestation without duality. That is clear. But in day-to-day living, I cannot escape my preferences, I cannot escape the splitting. So to come back to my initial point: yes, I sense the mind sustains the sense of being a separate individual by splitting life into a 'wanted' and 'unwanted' side, but this seems inescapable…? How can this ever resolve?

Answer: As Dogen said:

> 'Although everything has Buddha nature, we love flowers, and we do not care for weeds.'

Preferences occur, as do apparent differences; nothing but the absolute is absolute, and so, in day to day living, one man's weed appears as another man's flower. There is nothing that can or needs to be done about this.

This manifestation, as seen from the mind, will always function within the pairs of opposites. As such awakening is not an end to the 'show' as it appears now. With awakening comes the recognition that there is no separate character to awaken; which makes this whole awakening thing sort of a prank the Self plays on the Self. When the snake is projected into the rope, the rope is still the rope;

when multiplicity is projected on the One Screen it still is the One Screen. As soon as it is clear that there really is no separate character, preferences, likes and dislikes are no longer seen as attributes belonging to 'someone' who needs to resolve them. They're now recognized as some of the countless ways the One appears to itself; innumerable variations, but all on a single 'theme.'

In the body/mind the natural functioning expresses as certain characteristics, which can be labelled as preferences. We could for example say that certain flowers grow best in the shade, while others do better in direct sunlight. We could express this same idea, by saying that certain flowers prefer the shade, while others prefer the sun.

By exclusively identifying with the body/mind complex, and its undeniable preferences, an artificial idea of a personal self 'having' those preferences appears. But closer, closer yet, closer than close, is the centre from which the questions and preferences are seen. This centre is not a person, nor is it a thought or a state. We could point at it by calling it the Unknowable Knower who has room for all characters, thoughts and states. Because of its unconditional non-quality of limitless spaciousness, it has also been called 'pure and unconditional love.'

This 'something/no-thing' has actually no attributes – not even 'pure unconditional love' – and it's absolutely zero to the mind. There are no 'handles' on it and it cannot be reached, much like you cannot reach the place where you are.

All 'handles' are, as you pointed out yourself, steeped in duality; even the 'handle' of awakening. They are all mind-generated, and on closer inspection, it can be seen that the mind itself is duality in action. The mind splits the One into the many and even the concept 'I am' implies a 'you are.' It is this mind that introduces the question 'How to resolve the splitting?' without realizing that it is the splitting. It is mind itself that generates all opposites; from the most obvious to the most subtle. In the Tao Te Ching this splitting has poetically been called 'mutual arising.'

> *When everyone recognizes beauty as beautiful, there is already ugliness.*
> *When everyone recognizes goodness as good, there is already evil.*
> *'To be' and 'not to be' arise mutually;*
> *Difficult and easy are mutually realized;*
> *Long and short are mutually contrasted.*

And in the same book it says:

> *The nameless is the origin of heaven and earth.*
> *Naming (the mind) is the mother of the ten thousand things.*

Like fire cannot escape heat, the mind cannot escape the splitting it is. In the same way the 'I' cannot escape preferences, as preferences are part of the conceptual 'I' structure. If there is an escape option at all, it is in the realization that no escape is needed, as this 'I' is not all that I AM.

'Naming' is the origin of all apparent duality and it is the way the game is played. Without this context there would be no appearance of play at all; but regardless of how it appears, the 'origin of heaven and earth' itself is never divided. Everything is already perfectly resolved in the Single Source from which this manifestation arises and to which it returns.

ᘒ ᘒ ᘒ

As the rivers flowing east and west
Merge in the sea and become one with it,
Forgetting they were ever separate streams,
So do all creatures lose their separateness
When they merge at last into pure Being.
There is nothing that does not come from him.
Of everything he is the inmost Self.
He is the truth; he is the Self supreme.
You are that, Shvetaketu; you are that!

From: The Chandogya Upanishad

4. My mind is always complaining

Question: I am frustrated with not being able even to have a split second experience of the Self. My mind is always complaining about this and that.

When it is hot it complains about the heat and when the body does not feel too well it complains. So this complaining goes on all the time. I don't blame the body and mind for complaining because there is no escape from the tyranny of life. It doesn't mean I am not happy. I am often happy when everything is going my way, according to plan, but otherwise I have a flood of angry thoughts. The mind is the way it is, it can't stop. I think you know what I mean. Is there any way out of this dream, which seems very real while it lasts?

Answer: Your frustration is understandable, because you're looking in the wrong direction. The Self is not an experience; it is the experiencing. Like sight can see but never be seen, the experiencing can experience, but not be experienced. You are that experiencing.

This understanding already comes through in your words. Who is it that sees the mind jump around? Since it sees the mind's activity it must be beyond the mind. There is no escape from the tyranny of life because there is no 'you' that is bound by it.

Look inside to where there supposedly is an 'I.' Can you find it, or is it just more thought? And what is thought? Isn't it just mind again? There is no you to be happy or upset. There are just emotions arising and the mind labels them as positive or negative. This labeling seems to be done by an 'I' but truly it is nothing but mind also.

Relax into the seeing. Realize that all that arises is the seen. It comes, it lingers for a while and it's gone, but the seeing (the Self) remains.

The angry thoughts have no power. The power they apparently have comes from beyond them and from the mistaken belief that they are YOUR thoughts. Watch the thinking (you are the watcher), see how thoughts come up by themselves, and only after they have arisen, comes the thought that it is YOU who had this thought. Again, this is nothing but the next, self-arising, spontaneous thought.

Do not simply accept or reject this, but verify it. No one else can do it.

ல் ல் ல்

All there is is this. All there is is the seeing of this. Whatever that is... feeling warm, hearing a sound, sitting on a chair, feeling angry, feeling frustrated, all of these things are simply sensations but there is no fixed datum called me in here... just happenings.

Tony Parsons in Amsterdam, Saturday 27th July 2002
http://www.theopensecret.com/

5. Near death experiences

Question: In near-death experiences (NDEs) it is said that the soul sometimes leaves the body and sees the situation from above, noticing things that could never be seen from the body's perspective. If there is no separate self as Advaita teaches, how can there be a separate soul? In short, how does the concept of soul fit into a non-dual perspective? Who is it that sees from the ceiling in a NDE? How does seeing take place without a body?

Answer: The seeing you refer to does not automatically imply a separate soul. THAT which appears as everything can also appear as the seeing in a NDE. The next step that is often reported in NDEs is that there seems to be a perceived threshold, which the person having the experience considers as a point of no return. From the perspective of Advaita, going beyond that threshold is simply the final step, after which the illusion of one's separate individuality merges back into the oceanic Self.

I answer this question because I do not want to give you the idea that I am avoiding a difficult topic, but I also would like to remind you that the mind is very clever and able to produce endless questions. The ultimate answer is not in the mind; the mind lives in (and by the grace of) the ultimate answer.

There is no way that thinking can take you beyond thinking. From this the mind may conclude that this is very difficult or just mumb-jumbo, used to avoid tough questions.

As always I point back to THAT which is aware of the mind. It is prior to thought and beyond simple and complex. It is THAT which expresses via the mind as the thought 'I Am.' But YOU ARE before that thought can arise. Stay with that, and questions distracting you from the true essence will dissolve.

၈၀ ၈၀ ၈၀

All bodies are just instruments. All bodies are only temporary. They have birth. They have death. The indweller of the body is permanent. That is the Atma, the one Self. That is you. That is the real you. You are the immortal Self, not the body.

~ Sai Baba ~

6. What bothers me about Advaita

Question: Hello – thank you for the book. I have a question that continues to bother me about Advaita. How do we know that what we refer to as awareness is not a function of this brain?

Although Advaita says that all arises within awareness, isn't it also true that this awareness that I am will disappear at my death?

Please help with any suggestions. It just seems clear to me that without this brain there would be no awareness for this body/mind I refer to as me.

Answer: As to the 'how' of your question I have no real answer. I also don't know how the heart beats, how the cells divide and renew and how the metabolism works. I know we can describe these processes to a certain extent, but that seems to be more about what is happening, rather than how it is happening. How there can exist anything at all, especially consciousness, is (literally) mind-blowing.

You mix two things together; that what I point to as 'Pure Awareness' and 'personal awareness.' The term Pure Awareness is, as said throughout the book, a conceptual pointer to the 'Livingness' that allows me to do the pointing. What you call 'the awareness that I am' which might or might not disappear at the moment of death (see the previous question about NDEs) is how this Animating Energy expresses via the brain. The primal thought is 'I Am'. This is after you have acquired the words to think this, but before that thought can arise, you are. This 'Primal You' is not the personal character which identifies itself as a body/mind organism. It is the energy that 'powers' this whole manifestation.

Compare this Animating Energy to electricity, which expresses as light via a light bulb. The light bulb may consider its wiring as that which supplies the light. When the bulb 'hears' about this undying electricity, it may say, 'Yes, but when this wiring inside me finally gives out, the light disappears and that will be the end of me.' If this lamp would see that the light originates in the electricity and not in its wiring, it would recognize this as its true nature; That which enlivens it and That which is not affected by the end of the lamp.

All I can suggest is to find out how real this 'me' is that might die. The certainty that you are not the body has to come and burn away the doubts. Find and recognize 'the electricity' that lights up 'your' wiring. This recognition cannot be given to you as it takes the 'you' you think you are away. See if this 'you' that supposedly does the thinking can be found apart from thought itself. See if there really is a 'you' that does the thinking and the living. If it cannot be found, then who is going to die?

As long as you believe yourself to be limited to the body/mind organism, instead of seeing that you are the Animating Energy, you will be like the lamp and you will sell yourself short.

∞ ∞ ∞

4-14: My friend, there is no cause for disquietude since you are not the body. You are imperishable and eternal, then why do you cry?

Rest in peace.

Space-like, immortality-giving knowledge absolute am I.

From the 'Avadhut Gita' by Dattatreya,
translated by Hari Prasad Shastri

7. Is this witnessing?

Question: I was totally involved in an argument although I had 'decided' I would try to watch the role-playing at this meeting. I was later annoyed with myself that I was so involved arguing etc that I totally forgot everything.

When talking to a friend she said, 'But you were "witnessing" because you remembered it.' I felt I was in the Maya and in the involvement and had forgotten who I was or am. What I wanted to know is, is this witnessing?

Answer: Witnessing is not something you do. It is the realization that there is an alive awareness of all that's going on. Witnessing is always present, and the realization of it is what is pointed to, both here and in the book 'Awakening to the Dream.'

See, even when you are totally absorbed in an activity or thought, something is aware of this. It is this awareness that allows you to know that – as you say – 'I was so involved arguing etc that I totally forgot everything.' Something has noticed this, otherwise you would not be able to recall and report it. It is also aware of the idea that there might be a 'you' trying to do the witnessing. This 'you' or ego seems to have awareness, but in reality there is awareness of the you/ego.

The recognition of this witnessing presence is not something to be practised by an apparent separate entity. It is the impersonal recognition of and by the ever-present One-Self-Aware-Reality.

So yes, the witnessing was there when you thought it

was not, because something was aware of the apparent time and space in which you thought you did not do witnessing. In the end there is no separate 'you' to do it. The comings and goings of the 'you' that tries to witness are being witnessed.

ᕿ ᕿ ᕿ

217: HOW CONFUSION ARISES WITH REGARD TO THE WITNESS. Suppose you are the witness to a particular thought. A little later, you remember that thought and you say you had that thought some time ago – assuming thereby that you were the thinker when the first thought occurred, though you were then really the witness of that thought.

This unwarranted change in your relationship with a particular thought – from when the thought occurs to when you remember it – is alone responsible for the whole confusion with regard to the witness.

When you seem to remember a past thought, it is really a fresh thought by itself and it has no direct relationship with the old one. Even when you are remembering, you are the witness to that thought of remembrance. So you never change the role of your witnesshood, however much your activities may change.

From: 'Notes on Spiritual Discourses of Shri Atmananda', taken by Nitya Tripta (1952)

8. About addiction

Question: I don't want to bring this down to the level of an agony aunt column, but I do wonder if you have anything to say about addiction, perhaps putting it in a larger context.

I guess I am asking about cravings and obsessive behavior.

Answer: What came up when I considered your question was that the root problem of all problems is the sense of being a separate entity and being identified as the body/mind.

From this 'root' can grow a mighty tree with countless branches and leaves. Addiction is one of those growths and to work on such problems leaf by leaf, branch by branch is a daunting and never-ending task.

My suggestion is to go directly for the root. Find out that you are not the body/mind. If or when this becomes absolutely clear, the problem of addiction is gone. Addiction may or may not continue, but it is no longer 'your' addiction and 'your' problem.

The body/mind Wayne Liquorman was struck sober, but Nisargadatta was addicted to nicotine, and died from it. He did not consider his name, body or mind as his identity.

Addiction may be of the body, it may be of the mind and it is one of the ways awareness appears to itself.

That which you truly are is not addicted to anything. It is freedom itself and you are THAT.

∞ ∞ ∞

In truth that which you call freedom is the strongest of these chains, though its links glitter in the sun and dazzle the eyes.

And what is it but fragments of your own self you would discard that you may become free?

From: Freedom by Khalil Gibran

8. A False Sense of liberation

Question: Ramana Maharshi said that there is a false sense of liberation that aspirants reach that very few ever go beyond.

Would you comment on this line? It seems to point to 'Let's wait for the BIG awakening!' What is the false sense?

Answer: We have to remember that Ramana Maharshi's words were often part of a conversation and to interpret them without knowing the context in which they were spoken is tricky. So please keep this in mind when reading the response that came up.

Although I can find many Ramana quotes pointing to the exact opposite, this statement seems to suggest that there are individuals that can reach a future goal of enlightenment, while enlightenment shows that there never was an individual to reach anything. The gateless gate as Zen calls it.

Furthermore, if all there is is Oneness then, whether IT appears as clarity or as a false sense of liberation, makes no difference. Both positions are modifications in a Single Light, which – like a movie – appears on the screen of Awareness. Nothing can affect this contextual, space-like Awareness in any way. It is always present and can therefore never be reached or abandoned. Just like three-dimensional space cannot be reached or left by the objects that occupy it.

In the end it does not matter what Ramana, Zen, I or

anyone else has to say about it. All are concepts pointing to the non-conceptual knowing that is present prior to the mind. **It is the knowing that knows that you are** before it is conceptualized as the thought 'I Am.' The conviction that this is so has to come from the Sourceless Source, out of which everything (including this conceptualizing) arises.

ᕓ ᕓ ᕓ

39: Only so long as one considers oneself bound, do thoughts of bondage and Liberation continue. When one enquires who is bound the Self is realized, eternally attained, and eternally free. When thought of bondage comes to an end, can thought of Liberation survive?

From: 'Forty Verses on Reality' by Sri Ramana Maharshi,
translated by Arthur Osborne

9. Time tested rules

Question: Perhaps all senses of liberation, whether true or false, are at best only temporary. 'This too shall pass.'

I don't see any reason why 'awareness' itself should be excluded from this 'time tested' rule.

Answer: Awareness is just a word to point at the nameless IT. Unconditional Apple Pie would do as well.

All that falls under 'time tested rules' will come and go. But THAT in which it comes and goes, does by itself not come and go. Coming and going is of time and space. THAT from which both time and space arise, is prior to manifestation and untouched by it. Even the mind's own logic dictates this to be so.

When we perceive a universe with time and space, we also perceive cause and effect. When there is cause and effect there must be a first cause. This first cause must by itself be uncaused; otherwise it would not be the first cause. It therefore has no beginning. If it has no beginning it has no end and qualifications such as before and after, or front and back cannot apply to it. Without these criteria it is outside of – or prior to – the dimensions of space and time.

Nothing said or written can be IT and yet, everything is IT. Just like all objects appearing in space simultaneously are and are not the space they appear in, as beyond the subatomic level they 'collapse' into energy/space. In the same way, all that appears in IT/Awareness dissolves into IT/Awareness.

Liberation is when THAT/Pure Awareness, which has no beginning or end, and which does not come and go, is recognized by THAT as 'your/Its' True Identity.

*After I wrote this, someone made me aware of Thomas Aquinas 'Reasons in Proof of the Existence of God.' (1270).

In this text he uses similar arguments to prove the existence of God, or the first Unmoved Mover of all that moves. His words are the basis for lots of discussions between proponents and opponents of his arguments. Since his ideas can be argued, they do not constitute a final or real proof. If this is of interest to you, and you have access to the internet, you can find lots of web pages dedicated to this discussion.

ဢ ဢ ဢ

Things are not what they seem; nor are they otherwise.

~ Lankavatara Sutra ~

10. Nothing happens

Question: Really enjoyed all the excerpts and newsletters. Your explanation is profound and understood, perhaps only because I have been reading about the awareness/observer for so long. Unfortunately, I get in this loop of my mind trying to go beyond my mind, out of the ego.

So nothing happens. I decided to put off the awareness until I die! Otherwise it is too painful and I cannot cope with this life.

Answer: The main thing to see is that there is no 'I' to either get in or out of the loop. It is also not 'your' mind it is just mind. Nor is it you that has to see this. There is just seeing without someone doing the seeing. The hierarchical structure of our language demands there be an 'I' to do the seeing, and then it is forgotten that this 'I' itself is nothing but language/thought. The 'I' in 'I think' has as much substance as the 'it' in 'it rains.'

Observe and see that thoughts simply come up, without a 'you' doing the thinking, and they will no longer be seen as problematic. It is just what is, complete in itself and in no need of alteration or modification.

It can also be seen that something is aware of the mind's activity; otherwise it could not be reported. This Awareness cannot be an object to itself. It is the knowing that cannot be known and the seeing that cannot be seen. Realizing that THAT is what you truly are is not an experience for some one; it is the inexperience-able experiencing itself and You Are THAT.

Waiting for this to become clear is again just self-arising and spontaneous thought which is simply the way IT appears to itself and not 'you' not getting it. Everything is IT and you are THAT. It is not about something that you can put off until you die; IT is what you truly are, just like the wave and the ocean are nothing but 'One Water.' This is so, even when IT is expressing AS an apparent separate you and everything else that appears; including stars, birds and doubts, whether or not this is really so.

As you said 'nothing happens.' It is as it is and there is no need to wait for an experience. All experiences come and go, but THAT which is aware of them does not come and go. It is the Aware Space in which all arises and dissolves, just like yesterday's thoughts came up and dissolved again.

There is no you that has a life to cope with. Life is simply 'living' life and IT does it also *as* 'you.' Painfulness may arise, pleasure may arise, but THAT in and to which it arises is the uncaused joy that knows no opposites. IT is the still heart at the centre of the storm; IT is the self-shinning mirror, unaffected by whatever is reflected in it. You are THAT.

๛ ๛ ๛

No effort is needed for that aliveness to be. Nobody is doing aliveness. Is anybody doing sitting on a chair? Thinking is oneness thinking 'I don't get where this is going', or 'this is too simple'. All is simply aliveness, oneness, being. It cannot be taught or achieved. Who is apart from being to achieve being? Who can lose or gain this when this is all there is? Resisting oneness is oneness resisting. Seeking oneness is oneness seeking itself.

Tony Parsons on his website: http://www.theopensecret.com/

11. The final pinnacle of evolution

Question: Is this awakened 'state' the ultimate reality, the final pinnacle of evolution? How can this be known to be certain, that there is nothing more than this?

How can certainty be there that this is it?

Answer: Evolution is from the relative level of existence. IT/the Ultimate is not the pinnacle of evolution, but it is THAT from and in which apparent evolution arises. Within the framework of the dream of existence, where the illusions of time and space apply, evolution could go in all directions.

Perhaps the ability for telepathy could evolve, or we could discover faster-than-light travel, or how to teleport and find the secret to being physically young for 10,000 years. 'Beam me up Scotty!'

You write: 'How can certainty be there that this is it?' THIS is its own certainty. It cannot be known by someone but is the very knowing itself. Evolution does not apply to the infinite. All apparent evolution appears in time/space and is a play in and on the silent background from which it all bubbles up. Whatever comes up does not affect IT, like the movie screen remains unaffected whether a Star Trek movie or 'Gladiator' appears on it.

Like space itself, IT remains forever unaffected by what appears in it, and like space it will still be there when appearances dissolve back into it. If even the metaphor space remains itself indescribable, how much more so does this apply to THAT for which the space metaphor is used? And, just as it is with space, the dualistic concepts of certain/uncertain, knowing/not knowing, do not apply. IT is not something complicated, but nevertheless IT is incomprehensible. IT is all pervasive, timeless, ever-present and pure.

All these descriptions are mere pointers, as IT cannot be made into a concept. IT is closer than close, the centre from which all emanates, including the sense of being an individual with questions. IT is what you are, THAT which appears AS you, not something you can get. Like an arrow, able to point in all directions but not to itself. This is IT and you are THAT.

൚ ൚ ൚

A thing can prove only itself. Seeing proves only seeing. Hearing proves only hearing etc, etc. Similarly I prove only myself.

From: 'Notes on Spiritual Discourses of Shri Atmananda', taken by Nitya Tripta (1952)

12. Looking for my bliss

Question: Josephs Campbell's 'follow your bliss' has touched my heart, and yet, as much as I continue to look for my 'bliss,' I have not found it in a livelihood which would make my heart sing.

Are you suggesting that this is just 'what is' and that there is nothing I can do to find my life's work and actually earn a living doing that? There is frustration, anxiety and great debt right now; do I have any choice in the matter?

Answer: As I am not familiar with Joseph Campbell's 'follow your bliss' I cannot say anything about the contents of the book. This phrase seems to suggest that there is a separate you that can either follow or not follow her bliss. From the non-dual perspective this concept doesn't make much sense.

It is not so much that you cannot do anything, but that there is no separate you to do it. Everything done or not done is how IT/God appears to him/herself. The sense of separation, the sense of being an individual, is also IT appearing AS the apparent individual. When seeing many beautiful statues and ornaments all made of go(l)d, you can either focus on all the different shapes or notice that in essence it is all One Substance.

Everything that happens is an encouragement to see what it is that really lives 'your' life. If there really was a 'you' in control of 'your' thoughts and feelings, would this you ever have an unhappy thought or emotion? Again I am not suggesting that you are helpless, but that there is no you to be helpless.

The problems you describe are painful. The more there is willingness to be with WHAT IS, regardless of what it is, the more there will be peace. The bliss you're looking for gets obscured by the very looking, by wanting things to be different. As Chuang-Tzu said:

Happiness is the absence of striving for happiness.

The more we want things to be different the greater the pain. We seemingly run into contradictions here, because if there is a wish for things to be different, then that is the way it is and that might be welcomed.

Bliss is not something you get, but it is what you essentially are. It is the Aware Space in which the opposites of pain and pleasure arise. It is the deep silence from which everything comes forth and into which it dissolves again. It is the uncaused joy, unaffected by troubles, as a mirror is unaffected by what it reflects. You are THAT, You are the mirror in which both the 'you' and the current pain arises.

If this is recognized and accepted by no one, there is peace. Suffering may continue or a way out may open up on the relative level. That what you truly are is Bliss itself and there is no one to follow or get it. It is simple and pure being. You Are That.

෨෨ ෨෨ ෨෨

Happiness is like a butterfly:
the more you chase it,
the more it will elude you,
but if you turn your attention
to other things,
It will come and sit softly on you shoulder.

~Thoreau ~

13. Today there is freedom!

Question: Awareness is consciousness already, without any 'doing', but it doesn't know it! That's why there is suffering, isn't it?

Answer: There is no division between the knower and the known; there simply is knowing. This splitting up into knower and known is mind. And is it not clear by now, that the mind – the great pretender – does not get IT?

IT = undivided.
Mind = division.

The sufferer is created via the mind's identification with objects, be they the body, thoughts, or emotions. The suffering appears via the mind's splitting the One into the many. Next it starts labelling certain 'parts' of the game as desirable, automatically putting the remainder in the category of the undesirable. From here it starts on a fruitless endeavour of turning to the right, in an attempt to get rid of the left. Sometimes it seems to work and it calls this happiness, sometimes it is clear that it does not work, and it calls this suffering.

Seeing through this endless loop is in a sense being out of the loop. Herein is uncaused joy without an opposite. Because it has no opposite the mind (being division) cannot touch it. For this reason it is also pointed at as no-thing-ness, as it is nothing to the mind.

Question: But Awareness which is not self-aware is just nothingness. Meaningless. Emptiness.

Answer: There is truth in this statement, but it is rather nihilistic. It is the same sort of truth that declares a great wine to be nothing but fermented grape juice. It is like saying of a great work of art that it is nothing but smeared paint on canvas, and that music is nothing but a collection of noises. All true, but you surely feel that something is lacking in such observations.

Awareness not being self-aware is one way of putting it, but Awareness IS Awareness just like light is light. The fact that light cannot shine upon itself does not mean that it is darkness. The fact that sight is invisible to itself does not cause blindness. It only means that it is not an object to itself. It just IS. Self-evident, or as is often said about Awareness: Self Shining.

Really, if there was a 'clarity formula', graspable by the mind, I'd gladly make it available to you and all, but it is not. For 'the answer' look into 'your own' intrinsic everyday awareness, which sees concepts such as suffering, meaninglessness, and emptiness come up and disappear again.

If at all possible, turn away from all objects, including the mind-generated ones; turn around 180 degrees and see from where the light shines that lights up all objects and concepts. Do not expect a conceptual answer, but see what it is that makes all concepts 'visible.'

This instant there is a choice presented; just choice, no chooser, just as when these words are presented there is reading, but no reader. This phantom only appears when one stops the reading to declare 'I am reading.'

The mind jumps into its battle station and starts to throw out all kinds of 'yes but's.' You can follow this 'leader/imposter' who tries to usurp the throne of identity, or you can say 'No thank you. Not today. Today I'm staying home. "I" see what you're trying to do and "I" do not go along with this charade. Today there is freedom!'

∽ ∽ ∽

Realize that what you are cannot be born nor die and with the fear gone all suffering ends.

~ Nisargadatta Maharaj ~

14. What is it that makes the ONE appear to be many?

Question: Everyone says that it's consciousness that seems to appear as everything. I want to ask what is it that makes this consciousness... this oneness... manifest itself in so many forms. What is it that makes the One appear to be many?

I would like to know your reasons for it. Please don't speak from books because I've read many myself. Tell me what you know. That which you have experienced.

Answer: The One appearing AS the many is Self-Originating. It is the Causeless-First-Cause, the Sourceless-Source. It is THAT which brings forth time and space and is itself prior to time and space. It has no why, nor when, nor location, and IT IS, without a reason for being. We could say IT is itself the very reason for all being and non-being.

No label sticks to it and therefore it has been called the void. Even calling it the void is again a label and again just words. Whatever I answer will be words and apparently you have found words to be unable to convey the answer you're looking for.

You ask what my experience is. When you read the book 'Awakening to the Dream' and the answers in the other newsletters, you'll find that I do not call this 'understanding' an experience for someone, but point to the realization that there is no individual who can have such an experience.

IT is not something that can be put into plain words,

so no one can tell you what IT is. It is like asking about the taste of an apple: it cannot be explained. Not because it is something complex, but because words are always symbols for something; they are never the thing itself.

In the case of the apple, words can point you to an apple seller or an apple tree, but the tasting can only be done by you. With your question there can only be a pointing back to the Livingness that allows 'you' to ask this question.

One taste from 'the apple of enlightenment' will dissolve the taster and only taste remains.

∾ ∾ ∾

One matter, one energy, one Light, one Light-mind,
Endlessly emanating all things.
One turning and burning diamond,
One, one, one.

From: 'The Rumi Collection', Andrew Harvey

15. Why?

Question: I want to ask a simple question: why are we born into this world and why do we die?

Answer: The simplest answer is 'why not.' As this might not be very helpful, here is a bit more.

The question may sound reasonable but is in fact not very meaningful. You are asking for the meaning of life while everything that has meaning is a relative position within life.

It is like asking 'Where is space located?' whereas everything that has a location occupies a relative position within space. We could say that the location of space is space and that the meaning of life is life.

I would suggest that you first inquire 'who' you really are, before attempting to answer 'why' you are.

As soon as the 'who question' is answered, the 'why question' will dissolve.

൭൭ ൭൭ ൭൭

What's left without thought? Isn't there still an awareness of being present?

KNOW I AM – the pure Being in whom ALL the manifestation is appearing.

'Sailor' Bob Adamson on his website at: http://members.iinet.net.au/~adamson7/index.html

16. Is there an even playing field for all?

Question: Some actors in the play will awaken to the dream while others will not.

Does the Self cast some people in a role that precludes the possibility of Awakening or is there an even playing field for all?

If realizing our unreality is desirable, does this suggest a purpose to the game or is our state of awareness of no real significance in the big picture?

Answer: When I use the metaphor of the actor I always mean the One playing all the roles. What you call the actors is what I call the different roles or masks of the One Self.

These 'masks' will never wake up; it is always the One waking up to itself. This waking up reveals that there is no separation anywhere and thus no separate individuals with either relevant or irrelevant states of awareness.

Realizing this or not realizing this are both the One Self appearing as this cosmic play. In this game, Awakening may seem desirable and to be the game's purpose, but realization has no special merit.

Whether waking or dreaming, it is all THAT. Like many different ornaments all made of gold. Whatever form or shape gold assumes, it is always nothing but go(l)d. No ornament can become more true to its essence by changing shape, nor can a seeker become more THIS by changing her/his role to finder. I understand that it may seem so, but this is itself the illusion, which, of course, is again only another modification in Awareness or in the way IT appears to itself.

There is only THIS and no one to get IT, but (and here is the good news) also no one to be excluded from the party.

∾ ∾ ∾

But now a great thing in the street
Seems any human nod,
Where shift in strange democracy
The million masks of God.

From: Gold Leaves, a poem by G.K.Chesterton

17. Is being good or bad of any relevance?

Question: Your book is a consolation as well as a provocation. Nobody can be enlightened, nor be awakened. A mask or role can be awake or not in the dream, but that is not relevant, I understand.

But tell me please, IT being the actor, is it of any relevance to strive? For 'I' am not striving, but the One Self acting as me. Is being good or bad of any relevance? If the One Self plays all the roles, Gandhi but Saddam too, are its actors puppets so to say?

Answer: Relevance is a relative term within the game of life. Apparent events, actions, thoughts and deeds certainly have their value, just as pawns have relevance within the confines of the game of chess.

The word relevance has the same basis as the words 'relative' and 'relating.' Relating is from this to that, between such and so, but totality cannot relate to anything, because there is nothing outside IT to relate to.

Totality has no relevance, but it includes it as part of the game and within this game striving may appear; there is just no separate self which can choose to either strive or not strive.

Any move, each decision, every thought, all action or inaction, is a modification in the way Awareness appears to itself.

To say that Gandhi and Saddam are puppets is one way of putting it, but in truth, there are no individuals either used as puppets, or independently controlling 'their' lives;

there is only life living life as the apparent individuals.

Seeing that IT is One Substance, we cannot find a difference between the form and the substance. Just as it is not possible to separate the form of the statue from the stone from which it has been crafted. The form is the substance, the substance is the form.

All this is IT. IT is all this.

ഗ ഗ ഗ

Die while you're alive
And be absolutely dead.
Then do whatever you want:
It's all good.

Bunan, 17th Century Japanese Zen Master

18. The ultimate non-dual reality

Question: In your book you say that Pure Awareness is the ultimate non-dual reality. How could this be? Does awareness not need something to be aware of and does this not mean that awareness is dualistic?

Answer: Good point, but in the same book you'll also find: 'Zoom out, and Awareness and its content unify in a Self-luminous singularity about which nothing can be said or known for the simple reason that anything said or known is part-and-parcel of this singularity.'

The apparent duality of Awareness and its objects is a mind-generated division. If there is awareness, so goes the reasoning, there must be something else to be aware of. The mind, or the thinking process, can by its very nature only operate in the pairs of opposites – or in a gradient mix of them – such as hot/cold, high/low, good/bad, subject/object, observer/observed and so on. However, Pure Awareness/Consciousness is the whole enchilada; it is the clouds, the birds and the sky... every-thing, as well as no-thing.

Let us compare Awareness to something simple like a stick. We can say that the stick has a centre and two ends. The centre and the two ends are a way of conceptually dividing the stick – which can be great for practical purposes - but in actuality the centre and the two ends have no existence apart from the stick. We cannot remove them from the stick to end up with two separate ends without a centre, or a centre without two ends. The same goes for Awareness; conceptually it can be divided in the perceiver, the perceiving and the perceived, but in fact it constitutes a single indivisible whole.

Perhaps it works better for you when we drop the words Awareness/Consciousness and replace them with IT. IT is not so easily turned into a dualistic picture by the mind. In clarity IT recognizes itself as all there is and all there is not; uncaused and self-shining. There is nothing apart from Pure Awareness, this One Substance, this One Taste or this Single Source... no matter how it may appear to the mind.

In Hindu terms: All there is, is Brahman; Brahman is all there is. IT is absolute Oneness, magically disguised as multiplicity. This is the mystery; THIS is IT.

Below you'll find some words from the 'Yoga Vasistha' emphasizing this in different ways.

ल∞ ∞ ∞

Even as heat is to a fire, whiteness to a conch-shell, firmness is to a mountain, liquidity to water, butter is to milk, coolness to ice, brightness is to illumination, oil is to mustard seed, flow is to a river, sweetness is to honey, ornament is to gold, aroma is to a flower – the universe is to consciousness. The world exists because consciousness is, and the world is the body of consciousness. There is no division, no difference, and no distinction. Hence the universe can be said to be both real and unreal: real because of the reality of consciousness, which is its own reality, and unreal because the universe does not exist as universe, independent of consciousness. (p.50)

The mountains, the forest, the earth and the sky - all these are but infinite consciousness. That alone is the very being of all, the reality in all. (p.68)

As all things are equally indwelt by intelligence, so at all times in every way the uncreated is all, the self of all. We use the expression 'all things': it is only a figure of speech, for only infinite consciousness or Brahman exists. Just as there is no division between a bracelet and gold, there is no division between the universe and the infinite consciousness. The latter alone is the universe: the universe as such is not infinite consciousness, just as the bracelet is made of gold but gold is not made of bracelet. (p.71)

The self remains itself even when the energies of the world throw up endless diversities on the surface of the ocean of consciousness. There are no independent entities in this world known as 'body' etc. What is seen as the body and what are seen as notions, the objects of perceptions, the perishable and the imperishable, thoughts and feelings and their meaning - all these are Brahman in Brahman, the infinite consciousness. (p.271)

From: 'The Concise Yoga Vasistha' ISBN 0-87395-954-X

19. What is the Dark Night of the Soul?

Question: Some modern spiritual masters, at least the ones I'm familiar with, somehow make enlightenment sound like something simple and natural, something that just happens one day when there is enough maturity. With the exception of Douglas Harding, who speaks of 'The Barrier', as a very painful and heart-wrenching experience that, according to him, almost invariably precedes true awakening. (Thaddeus Golas also says something of the same sort, although not so clearly, and Ramesh Balsekar tells of a state bordering on psychosis, of 'almost going mad' before 'the understanding happened'). Few other writers speak of the subject.

Yet, in the Christian tradition, the Dark Night of the Soul, or the Cloud of Unknowing, is a recurrent theme in the writings of the great mystics.

What do you think about this? What is the Dark Night of the Soul, in your view, or experience?

Answer: Enlightenment is basically simple. The problem with saying this is that the mind may respond with, 'If it is so simple, why don't I get it?' The answer to that is that there is no one to get it. All questions and all answers are mind, and the truth of what you are is prior to the mind. It's like seeing your face for the first time in a mirror. You did not suddenly get it and nothing changed; it was there all along. Your 'Original Face' is also already and always present. It cannot be seen, as it is the very seeing; it cannot be known, as it is the very knowing.

While seeking there might appear to be a process to uncover this 'original face'. This apparent process may include a 'dark night of the soul', but there are no fixed rules as to how awakening is supposed to come about. When the 'gateless gate' is passed and clarity is present, it is seen that nothing can be isolated as the cause for the realization of the Uncaused.

For many people enlightenment is synonymous with either a mystical experience or a state achievable through personal effort or acceptance. In the chapter 'Blinded by the Light' (Chapter 18 in 'Awakening to the Dream') I recall such a mystical experience. It was indeed preceded by a deep depression and at the time I equated the ensuing mystical experience with enlightenment.

Currently I do not ascribe to this point of view and would say that – if there is something we want to label as enlightenmen – it has to be the recognition that there is no one to be enlightened; that awakening is about freedom from the person rather then freedom for the person and that it is not an experience, but the experiencing itself.

'Freedom from the person' is often translated into the idea that we should rid ourselves of our ego. When this concept is seen for what it is, it turns out to be nothing but the ego illusion itself. The futile effort to rid oneself of one's ego can cause exhaustion and frustration and may feel like a 'dark night of the soul.'

However, such a painful experience is not mandatory as awakening can also happen without such a struggle; there might be a gentle letting go, or the penny may suddenly drop. Regardless of how it will happen, it is the end of seeking as well as the end of the seeker. No future goal, no one to be present, just Presence.

ᗡᗡ ᗡᗡ ᗡᗡ

The cold hard facts are: There is no difference between a 'sage' and a 'seeker'– they are both appearances in that which you really are – ONE without a second – pure intelligence energy (Awareness) – BE what you are, you cannot really be anything else, though at times you may think so (both – mind clouds).

'Sailor' Bob Adamson on his website at: http://members.iinet.net. au/~adamson7/index.html

20. Is awareness dependant on a body/mind?

Question: OK, Awareness is all there is, it's the clouds up there, it's the sound of the cars outside, it's this body, thoughts, the chair...

Why does it take the specific point of view, specific locality of THIS body/mind (which it is not exclusive to) rather than say the chair or whatever?

Is Awareness dependent on a body/mind to reveal itself?

Answer: The short answer: it is not the person (the localized perspective) that can experience the infinite; it is the infinite that experiences the person. All forms are of One Substance, just as the waves on the ocean are all 'made' of water, yet water is not 'made' out of waves. The wave is the localized perspective in this metaphor. As long as the water 'waves' there is the apparent individual expression of such waves. As long as the One Substance 'peoples' there is the apparent individual expression of people.

The longer version: the form does not exist separate from the statue. The stone is the form, the form is the stone. The form may change, but the essence remains the same. Similarly, the unchanging and the changing, the localized and the non-local perspective, are but two conceptual ends of One Awareness.

Even when the localized perspective is present, there is something silently aware of this. This Awareness can itself not be localized. If we locate it between our ears and behind our eyes, as many do, then again, THAT which is aware of this remains as the non-objectifiable subject.

The best answer to the 'why' of your question is 'why not.' It is the way the game is played, between contraction and expansion; it is the nature of IT to appear as apparent diversity including persons. We could even say that a person *is* nothing but a localized perspective.

As the person IT may realize that his/her essence is not different from Totality, but as long as Totality/One Substance expresses as such, the local perspective will remain intact. This perspective can be recognized as a temporal occurrence, while the True Self is realized as eternal, non-local Presence.

IT is the sight in all eyes and the 'person' is the way IT sees from a certain perspective. In a mystical or peak experience, it is possible that the whole sense of localized awareness is swooped away – death is probably much like this – but for the daily functioning of the game it is not a very practical state to operate from.

You are not just this localized perspective, but THAT which is aware of and appears as this perspective. Awareness is not dependent on anything to reveal itself IT cannot be, because IT is all there is... and all there is not... Non-local, Uncaused and Self-Shining. You are That.

෨෨ ෨෨ ෨෨

Nothing is born and nothing dies. Nothing is happening. But this, as it is, invites the apparent seeker to rediscover its origin. When the invitation is accepted by no one, then it is seen that there is only Source... the uncaused, unchanging, impersonal stillness from which unconditional love overflows and celebrates.

Tony Parsons on his website: http://www.theopensecret.com/

21. Five in one

Hi Leo, hope you are well. Here are some questions if you may answer:

Question 1: Why do all enlightened teachers appear contradictory? Some say make an effort, others say effort is in the way, some say there should be a strong desire to find God, others say this desire is like any other desire, some say you have to meditate etc., others say there is nothing you can do about it. Whom to believe?

Answer: A big part of my life is and was spent in Amsterdam. The old city is built like circles within circles and regularly tourists get confused and ask directions. Often you can point them to the right, to the left as well as straight ahead crossing all the circles. Although these are three different directions, they'll all end up in the same place.

To the question whether to make an effort or not I would say that the belief in a separate entity is causing the apparent problem. By effort, seeking and doing, the separation and the idea of 'not being there yet' is affirmed. On the other hand I would not say that you should do nothing, but suggest having a look at whether there really is a separate you that does anything at all. If this separate 'I' cannot be found – and this has to be absolutely clear – the seeking and trying will drop away of their own accord.

Question 2: They also contradict each other on topics like reincarnation, karma, whether there is a 'soul' or individual entity (bubble), which survives after death. And the funny thing is that all of them sound so sure that what they say is true, others have got it wrong! And others say the same about them!

Answer: Nothing said or written is the truth; the most words can aspire to, is to point back to the source from which they arise. This happens in a million ways and it often depends on so many variables. If you ask me to point out Venus in the night sky at different times of the night you will observe me pointing in different directions. During daytime I will say that I cannot point to it at all.

I would not concern myself with karma, souls and reincarnation till the 'Who am I' question is answered. If after that answer there is still an ongoing interest in such matters, the answers will be more easily seen.

Question3: Recently read Tony Parsons' negating comments regarding Power of Now, earlier read Ramesh's negative comments about Osho, read Osho and Poonja's negative comments about Sai Baba – the cycle is endless. My question is – why can't one say after enlightenment that I still don't know, that it is all a mystery, that what I may say may still not be the truth? Why do they have an answer for every question?

Answer: Many of these people say that the ultimate truth cannot be objectified, that it cannot be grasped by the mind and that of course does not exclude their 'own' minds. Ramesh often says, 'What is said here is NOT the truth.' Tony Parsons points to contradictions he sees in certain teachings, but adds, 'Of course all of this confusion is as much an expression of oneness as the exposure of it.'

Question 4: What is the difference between you and me now, or to put it in another way, what is the difference between you now and what you were before enlightenment? If 'enlightenment' can be put as an event happening in time to a person, although you may not define it that way, but it seems everyone says that at such and such an age on a particular day enlightenment happened to me, e.g., Ramesh says it, Poonja said it and almost everyone else.

Answer: 'Before' is a relative term. There is this incomprehensible perception that nothing happened and that nothing is happening… ever! 'Before' there was the belief that awakening had to happen. Now the 'Isness' of IT takes the front seat. It is the Presence that has never been absent, which is why 'before' and 'after' no longer apply. To make talking possible I would say that 'before' I would believe that I used my mind; now there is just mind. Grammatically it is convenient to say 'I think' and 'I do' but there is this understanding that there is the appearance of thinking, doing, feeling and being without a 'me' doing the doing of all this. The difference between you and me is apparent. It is the One Source appearing as you and me. Whether it is recognized as such or not, whether it appears as impersonal clarity or as personal conditioning, it all comes directly from Source.

Question 5: And why does everyone start 'selling' enlightenment? Is it because there are so many takers and it is a convenient way to earn a living? I know many of the teachers lead a lavish lifestyle, have retreats at exotic places, fly around all expenses paid and adoration too!

Answer: Not every one comes out with this understanding.

Those who do – and are clear – know that they are selling water by the river. Instead of explaining anew the 'why' as it applies to this author, I'll include some text from the book 'Awakening to the Dream' below.

໑໑ ໑໑ ໑໑

Selling water by the river

'In my country, there is a proverb that may explain this. It says, 'The mouth has no choice but to speak of that which fills the heart.' Compare it to a man in love who cannot stop talking about his lady. His intention is not to convince his friends to go and court her; he simply is unable not to talk about her. He may even write her long love letters in which he says he can't find the words to express the love in his heart. When the lady in question shares his feelings, she understands what is meant, regardless of his admitted inability to accurately tell her his feelings.

In a similar way, this text is also about what cannot be captured in words; but that is not to say you won't get its message. It is not a message that is meant to convert you, but is simply that which fills my heart – and like most men in love- I love to share it. It would, however, be nearer the truth to say that it is that which shares itself – That being what we all have in common, the luminous, self-aware centre of our collective being.

Now we come to the disclaimer: You are advised to read carefully before swallowing any of the concepts contained in this book. They do not contain the truth, in the same way that the concept of water will not quench your thirst. Furthermore, they may be hazardous to your ego, your convictions, and your current values. Caution is advised in cases of extreme rigidity, since reading this book may lead to uncomfortable bending, stretching, or even to the annihilation of one's model of reality.

Of course, you have to take even this disclaimer with a pinch of salt, as it is one of the concepts it warns you about.'

22. The great paradox

Question: Is it possible that changing brain chemistry through meditation tapes, meditating, bodywork, or sudden trauma such as a fall or auto accident could lead to realization?

Answer: With your question you touch on the great paradox inherent in realization. Everything can lead to realization, yet nothing can lead to realization. The words 'lead to' seem to suggest that realization is a future goal to be reached by someone, while awakening reveals that both, future and a separate someone, are illusory.

Realization can be seen as the falling away of the illusion of time and separation. Since it is an illusion that falls away, there is in reality nothing that falls away and thus nothing that either leads to – or stands in the way of – awakening.

This may create a feeling of helplessness. So if that happens, I suggest you have a look and see what it is that is aware of this feeling of helplessness. Who or what is aware of everything including the body/mind and the questions that come up?

ல ல ல

Here are a few quotes from 'Awakening to the Dream' that address your question from different angles.

   * *This is not about a gradual progression to a future goal, but about a radical awakening to what is. No*

conditions have to be fulfilled for this to become clear. Self-realization can happen at any time for anyone.

* You don't need to do anything to 'become ready' for it. It will happen by itself and reveal that Awakeness is – and always has been – fully present. It will shine when it shines, and it will shift the attention from the content of Awareness to Pure Awareness itself.

* It may be silence from a sage or words from a shopkeeper. The surrender may come through agony or ecstasy. It can happen through an apple falling on your head; it can come from the smile of a child; or it can arise from deep inside as you walk along a beach at sunset or when you burn your finger on the stove. At any time, your sense of separation may dissolve to reveal the One beyond all duality.

* Enlightenment is not something difficult and remote, attainable only by an elite few. In fact, it is not attainable at all, but reveals itself through the removal of the illusion that there is an individual entity to take hold of it.

* There are no fixed rules as to how awakening should occur. The problem with preconceived notions about the much-coveted holy grail of truth and the packaging in which it should be delivered, is that such notions prevent the seeker from seeing that the liberation he is looking for is always fully present and instantly available.

23. Sadness and a steady diet of Advaita.

Question: There is this sadness that arises that feels like the loss of the story of Life, the story of me. Learning, growing, helping others. Is this part of what happens when exposed to a steady diet of Advaita?

Answer: There seems to be a sense that this sadness relates to a 'me.' In other words, there is someone experiencing a loss. This is still the story of 'me.' This 'me' is holding out on a small island of unhappiness and considers this better than having its cover blown completely.

I do not suggest that 'you' have to do some more work to get rid of the 'me' as this is just more of the same illusion. What is suggested here is recognizing that 'me' is one of the objects that arise in the Pure Awareness you are. This Awareness you are is not affected by what appears in it, just as a mirror is unaffected by what it reflects. To the mind this 'unaffected-ness' appears to be dreary. The mind wants to comprehend, but finds that It is not something it can take hold of. It cannot be perceived, as it is the very perceiving, it cannot be an experience as it is the very experiencing. This may make it seem empty and dull to the me/mind.

The invitation is to be the mirror and to consider the possibility of IT being empty and marvelous. What seems dull to the mind can be reframed as peace, and unaffected-ness can be reframed as total acceptance. The disappointment in the sadness can be seen as a total willingness to be with each feeling that arises.

Learning, growing and helping can still arise without

the idea that the destination is more important than the journey. What is more, the whole idea of journey and destination can drop away in favor of clear, simple and marvelous presence. There can still be helping when helping is required, but not from 'me' to another. It is just Self reaching to Self.

The mind is accustomed to have reasons to do something. It wants to 'grasp' meaning and to assign value, but when 'you' get the hang of it, when 'you' get in the swing of things, it is seen by no one, that THIS as it is, is its own fulfillment. It is seen that the reason for being is being itself and that, when manifest as sadness, it can be loved as such. Unconditional Love does not reject anything, not even a sense of loss. Letting those 'negative' feelings unfold and dissolve is the loving thing to do.

∾ ∾ ∾

And when the broken-hearted people
Living in the world agree,
There will be an answer, let it be.

For though they may be parted there is
Still a chance that they will see
There will be an answer, let it be...

~ Lennon & McCartney ~

24. How to play the game?

Question: I do understand that all that exists on the plane of a game that is played out here, but how do you personally keep playing this game knowing that nothing is relevant?

My understanding of all that is, is that it doesn't matter what toys you choose, as long as you enjoy the game and quit suffering, seeing that it's only a game and we are here to enjoy it. Is this the reality of things?

Answer: It is not I playing the game. There is just IT playing me. It is prior to relevant/irrelevant, which are just labels and modifications in the current of life. There is no me being the doer, there is just IT appearing AS you, me and everything else. Now there is typing going on. Now – as you – there is reading going on. Now the next thought appears like a bubble in a glass of champagne and action may or may not follow. It all happens spontaneously, not to or by us, but AS us.

Don't take this personal, because it cannot be personal.. The cosmic joke is that there is no you to understand, to choose toys, to enjoy the game or to quit suffering. There is just the One Energy taking all different shapes forms and vibrating into all possible patterns. There is simply IT appearing AS understanding without a 'you' doing the understanding. As I wrote in news letter number 15:

The 'I' in 'I think' (or the 'I' in 'I understand') has as much substance as the 'it' in 'it rains.'

Of course it is fine to use the word 'I', just as it is

convenient and correct to use the word 'it' as long as it is recognized for the abstraction it is.

You ask 'Is this the reality of things?' In the absolute sense there are no things. It is all the One appearing to herself in different shapes, forms and patterns. Just as a million statues made out of clay are all in essence the same One Substance. See through the illusion of differentiation and the One Substance is recognized as the true essence of all apparently different statues.

Just keep it simple. Non-dual... Not two... One!

Whatever 'you' think, it is IT thinking AS you.

Whatever 'you' do, it is IT doing it AS you.

ൟ ൟ ൟ

The nature of phenomena is non-dual,
but each one, in its own state,
is beyond the limits of the mind.

There is no concept that can define
the condition of 'what is'
but vision nevertheless manifests:
all is good.

Everything has already been accomplished,
and so, having overcome the sickness of effort,
one finds oneself in the self-perfected state:
this is contemplation.

From : 'Dzogchen: The Self-Perfected State' by Chogyal Namkhai Norbu.
Snow Lion Publications; (March 1996) ISBN: 1559390573

25. Don't worry, be happy

Question: Being IT, I love my manifestations, my wife, my children, the trees and mountains around me. I love my dog, my old-timer, my patients, the elegance and warmness of your book, I love also being old. I am, however, afraid of pain, troubled by world situations, hate Bush.

When I read some Advaita quotations, I think, I am totally wrong. My attitude should be one of indifference or perhaps better, there is nothing wrong with any manifestation, all being the way IT expresses itself to me (IT). The emotions, feelings, thoughts included. Please, where am I going wrong in these constructions?

Answer: You are truly IT. This does not mean that the person is IT, but that IT is the person. It is a small difference to see it like that, and yet it is a huge difference. It is like seeing that the wave is an expression of the ocean, rather than that the ocean is an expression of the wave.

The wave can recognize its true nature as nothing but ocean, even when it displays the properties of an apparent separate wave.

In the same way it can be seen that the 'wave/person' with all its preferences, likes and dislikes is but an expression of the Self. The character and its preferences can still appear. As long as the body/mind is present, its limitations and conditioning will keep on functioning to a certain degree. The conditioning may slow down when it is seen for what it is; nothing but another modification in the Awareness you are.

Remember, you cannot go wrong, as the apparent separate you is but an expression of the real YOU. If disagreement with Bush comes up, recognize it as part of the relative level where the game seems real; where one apparent character does not agree with an apparent other. Just let it be, disagree with a wink and a smile, and know it is all the One/You doing ITS dance.

As Meher Baba said:
'Don't worry, be happy.'

෩ ෩ ෩

For see!
The Self is in all beings,
And all beings are in the Self.
Know you are free,
Free of 'I',
Free of 'mine.'
Be happy.

The Ashtavakra Gita (15-6) translated by Thomas Byrom
Shambhala Publications ISBN: 1570628971

26. The real and the unreal

Question: What is meant in non-duality by 'It' being the real, and that which appears being the unreal?

Answer: The 'real' and the 'unreal' are terms often used in Advaita; the Hindu teachings of Non-duality.

The 'unreal' is that which is impermanent, or that what constantly changes, a.k.a. the objects in awareness. The 'real' is the unchanging context/awareness in which everything appears and dissolves again. There are metaphors involving the ocean or gold; both are powerful pointers. The ocean metaphor portrays the ocean as the 'real' and the separate existence of individual waves as the 'unreal.' In the go(l)d metaphor, the gold is the 'real' and the temporal ornaments/shapes IT assumes, make up the 'unreal.'

The famous Advaita story of seeing a snake on the garden path is also about this. All normal responses to being confronted with a snake arise, but – as it turns out – it is but a rope that has been mistaken for a snake. The rope is the 'real', the snake the 'unreal'.

The rope/snake story is often used to point to the illusion of the world. The world, seen as a collection of separate objects by a separate person, is the snake in the rope. The apparent snake/separation is a projection or 'unreal.' The 'real' is to know the whole manifestation as nothing but the One appearing to itself; appearing AS variation and apparent multiplicity.

In the end we have to leave the duality of real/unreal

behind as just two more concepts pointing to the clarity/ mystery from which they arise.

∽ ∽ ∽

All that you are attached to, all that you Love,
all that you know, some day will be gone.
Knowing this, and that the world is your mind
which you create, play in, and suffer from,
is known as discrimination.
Discriminate between the Real and the unreal.
The known is unreal and will come and go
so stay with the Unknown, the Unchanging, the Truth.

From: 'This: Poetry and Prose of Dancing Emptiness'
by H.W.L. Poonja (Papaji)1910 – 1997

27. Be the way you are

The following story landed one day in my mailbox. I don't know its origin or author, but it is a great pointer to total acceptance and simply being who or what you are... even when you're considered to be a crackpot.

〜 〜 〜

A water bearer in India had two large pots, each hung on the ends of a pole which he carried across his neck. One of the pots had a crack in it, while the other pot was perfect and always delivered a full portion of water.

At the end of the long walk from the stream to the house, the cracked pot arrived only half full. For two years this went on daily, with the bearer delivering only one and a half pots full of water to his house. Of course, the perfect pot was proud of its accomplishments, perfect for that for which it was made. But the poor cracked pot was ashamed of its own imperfection, and miserable that it was able to accomplish only half of what it had been made to do.

After two years of what it perceived to be bitter failure, it spoke to the water bearer one day by the stream. I am ashamed of myself, and I want to apologize to you. I have been able to deliver only half my load because this crack in my side causes water to leak out all the way back to your house. Because of my flaws, you have to do all of this work, and you don't get full value from your efforts,' the pot said.

The bearer said to the pot, 'Did you notice that there were flowers only on your side of the path, but not on the other pot's side? That's because I have always known about your flaw, and I planted flower seeds on your side of the path, and every day while we walk back, you've watered them. For two years I have been able to pick these beautiful flowers to decorate the table. Without you being just the way you are, there would not be this beauty to grace the house.'

28. Clarity, the senses and the brain

Question: I was wondering if you considered the state of clarity that you describe to be attributable to a functioning of sensory input into the brain.

Answer: When it is seen that all is ONE, it becomes hard to ascribe or not ascribe clarity to anything specific. It is like a piece of music played on a flute. Will one ascribe it to the flute (brain) or to the breath, the lungs, the flute maker, the flute player, the composer, or to the ears that translate the vibrating air into sound? We could go on and say it is the air that makes it all possible, which in turn is made possible by the conditions on our planet, which are possible because of the sun, and so on. It just depends on the angle it is approached from and the context thereby assigned.

Of course clarity requires a body/mind/brain to experience/express like this, but THAT which expresses AS all this is not dependent on anything. It is Self-Shining and prior to the temporal and spatial dimensions of this dream we call existence.

The real mystery – that there is anything at all – cannot be solved by the brain/mind as the brain/mind is but a part of (or an expression of) that mystery. See what happens when the mind is applied to the mystery of being. We can come up with elegant theories such as biological evolution. Before that we might perceive the formation of stars and galaxies. Still further back we can imagine 'first light' the 'big bang' and the beginning of time. Here linear logic has to stop. The mind cannot imagine 'before time' as before and after are qualities OF time.

Paradoxically the mystery is also pure simplicity, or an open secret. It is everything perceived, as well as the perceiving itself. It is not something the mind can grasp, but the mind can realize its own limitations here and let go. At this instant it can be understood that there is no one to understand. What remains is simply understanding; not the understanding OF the mystery, but of Being AS the mystery.

၈၀ ၈၀ ၈၀

'When my Beloved appears,
  With what eye do I see Him?'

'With His eye, not with mine,
  For none sees Him except Himself.'

~ Ibn al-'Arabi ~

29. Acceptance of what is

Question: My question has to do with the 'acceptance of what is,' as a pointer to our true nature. This total unconditional Acceptance implies no judgment/no categorizing/not labeling a situation as good or bad/ not controlling/not trying to change it. I perceive this acceptance as a total surrender to the way things are. When one tries to change 'what is' there is no acceptance, since by trying to change an attitude, circumstance or situation one is already labeling it wrong, incorrect, bad, harmful or evil (the continuous struggle in our minds between 'what is' and 'what should be.')

My dilemma is that it seems there is a thin line between this Total Acceptance and resignation/conformism/ apathy/quitting/giving up/and self-defeat. For example, I am a smoker; I have tried to stop a few times to no avail. Should I just accept myself as a chain smoker and stop trying to quit? I have a tendency to procrastinate: Should I accept that I am a chronic procrastinator and not try to change myself into a person who does things in a timely manner? Of course these examples can be extended to include perceived wrongnesses with relatives/friends/ communities and the world at large.

To accept means to admit, to consent, to acquiesce, to agree. How do I consent, agree or acquiesce to what I perceive is wrong in my life and in the life of others? Should I just smile and think it is the Dance of Shiva, Lila, a Dream or the Game of God (only a mirage)?

Answer: True-acceptance-of-what-is, is not something to be done by someone. When this concept is really looked into, it is found that there is no one to 'do' the accepting, yet it can be said that Total Acceptance is already fully present. Total Acceptance is another way of pointing to the context wherein everything appears; the Unchanging, or the True Source. IT rejects nothing, not even rejection. If IT would not allow/accept resistance, disagreement, or the attempt to change, IT would not qualify as TOTAL Acceptance.

The root of the confusion here is the assumption that there is an 'I' with 'my' life and that there are 'others' with 'their' lives, while it is no-thing but IT expressing AS life/apparent diversity. In this expression, there may be a hand touching a hot stove. The pulling away of this hand, when seen from the 'I' perspective, would then imply that 'I' do not accept the way it is, because 'I' remove 'my' hand from the cause of the discomfort. Seen from Source, the removal of the hand is what is happening, and it is fully accepted. This is the natural functioning within the expression of IT.

When changes have to be made, see if they can be made. Just check and perhaps see that it is not done by a separate 'me.' At that time it might also be seen that even this 'seeing' is not done by this apparent 'me.' The me-ing, the seeing; it is all the expression of 'Being.'

∽ ∽ ∽

When it's time to get dressed, put on your clothes. When you must walk, then walk. When you must sit, then sit.

Just be your ordinary self in ordinary life, unconcerned in seeking for Buddhahood.

When you're tired, lie down.

The fool will laugh at you but the wise man will understand.

~ Lin Chi ~

30. Other people's answers

Question: All the seeking has resulted in other people's answers (I realize I am talking as if I was a separate entity, but how else to ask the questions). Is there ever a place where I know for myself, as you know for yourself, or does one take it all on faith?

Answer: What I read here is the mind talking and being confused. Now let's do some mind/logic loops together.

The mind may be over-active, doubting or confused, but... there must be 'something' presently aware of this, which clearly and without confusion, recognizes confusion as confusion. In other words, something KNOWS this confusion and is not confused about what it knows. It recognizes doubt, and knows without a doubt, what doubt is.

This knowing is unknowable, just like sight cannot be seen. The knowing is the Mystery; IT is the True Self. It is not some-THING known by some one; IT is the very knowing itself. The mind does not 'know' how to deal with IT when it senses this. It cannot turn this knowing into the known, and is thus like an eye that franticaly turns in an attempt to see the source from which sight arises.

Seeing this clearly will not result in a 'me' or 'you' knowing IT, but there will be a willingness to be in 'not knowing.' Please think this through and it will be clear why the mystery of knowing can never be an object to itself. Can the sun throw light upon itself; can you kiss your own lips, or touch your fingertip with that very same tip? Seeing the logic of why it is not possible to know the Knowing-That-You-Are, the mind might give up and relax. It may still do its dance, it may continue for a while on its own momentum, but something unseen, sees all this. You ARE This Seeing Presence right now. It is THAT which knows the thoughts and THAT which allows you to report 'your' thoughts. It is THAT which remains, while thoughts come and go.

You know the reason why existence is pointless. You know it with your heart, not with the mind. The mind is looking for the point and for fulfillment. Here is some more logic, say that ultimate fulfillment is the point the mind is after and wants. Say that the mind gets it, then after that, what is the point then? The point of fulfillment IS fulfillment. The Awareness you ARE, IS Fulfillment. That is the reason why it is pointless; IT is IT'S own point. IT is not going anywhere, because IT is already everywhere. It is IT'S OWN FULFILLMENT. IT is complete even when from the limited perspective of the mind IT seems to appear as unfulfilled.

IT is not an experience, but the inexperience-able experiencing itself. Good moods, dark moods, doubts and clarity tumble by. Let them go, let them be. THAT which sees this IS the Mystery. You are THAT. The still centre of the storm, the heart of hearts, no goal, but FULFILLMENT itself

No words from another here, these are YOUR OWN WORDS, from Self to Self with Love.

ა ა ა

Consciousness is only ever having this conversation with itself. There is no 'other'. There is the appearance of 'many', but it's all the very same one, speaking as all these mouths, listening as all these ears, looking as all these eyes.

From: 'Already Awake' by Nathan Gill
Non-Duality Press, ISBN: 09547792-2-3

31. No purpose or meaning

Question: If there is no purpose or meaning to any of this other than to experience it, there is a certain despair that accompanies that aimless pointless existence.

Answer: Reflecting on this, it seems that purposelessness often equals delight. Dancing is not 'going' anywhere. We are not listening to music to reach the end of the song; we do not smell a rose in order to improve ourselves.

Watching clouds, seeing a bird soar, waves catching the sun's reflection on the ocean, and a billion stars scattered across the expanse of the sky; the sheer IS-ness of It All does not seem to demand – or to be in need of – a purpose beyond What IS.

∽ ∽ ∽

Someone asked, 'What was Bodhidharma's purpose in coming from the west?'

The Master said, 'If he had had a purpose, he wouldn't have been able to save even himself!' The questioner said, 'If he had no purpose, then how did the Second Patriarch manage to get the Dharma?'

The Master said, 'Getting means not getting.'

'If it means not getting,' said the questioner, 'then what do you mean by not getting?'

The Master said, 'You can't seem to stop your mind from

racing around everywhere seeking something. That's why the Patriarch said, 'Hopeless fellows – using their heads to look for their heads!' You must right now turn your light around and shine it on yourselves, not go seeking somewhere else. Then you will understand that in body and mind you are no different from the Patriarchs and the Buddhas, and that there is nothing to do. Do that and you may speak of 'getting the Dharma.'

From: 'The Zen Teachings of Master Lin-Chi'
translated by Burton Watson

32. Why do I ask the question?

Question: If knowing cannot be known, as sight cannot be seen, why do I ask the question? What compels Awareness to inquire of Awareness? Is it just Lila (a game/dance/dream)?

Answer: Dear ...
Why does a child try to see its own eyes?
Why does a cat look behind the TV to see where the bird on the screen has gone?
Why does a puppy chase its own tail?
And why do we humans chase our tales?

Perhaps to establish beyond all doubt the fruitlessness of such activity... Or perhaps just for the fun of it.

∽∾ ∽∾ ∽∾

Brahman has created the world not out of any desire or motive. It is simply His pastime, proceeding from His own nature, which is inherent in and inseparable from Him, as it is seen also in the world that sometimes a rich man or a prince does some action without any motive or purpose, simply out of a sportive impulse. Just as children play out of mere fun, or just as men breathe without any motive or purpose, because it is their very nature, just as a man full of cheerfulness when awakening from sound sleep, begins to dance about without any objective, but from mere exuberance of spirit, so also Brahman engages Himself in creating this world not out of any purpose or motive, but out of sporting or Lila or play proceeding from His own nature.

From: 'Brahma sutras' by Swami Sivananda

33. Who creates all the thoughts?

Question: A 'funny' question tortures me since a few days: Who creates all the thoughts whch are arising??? Where do they come from? If there is no I (and indeed 'I' cannot find it when I look) and life just 'happens', if there is no time and no space, how then do things develop? (It is a little bit difficult to me to explain what I mean in English.) If there is no beginning and no end, because all that is is THIS, who or what is creating this? Or is it self-creating? I hope you can understand what I mean.....

My mind is like an endless CD! Questions after questions after questions - and if I tell myself: this is only mind-play; it yet doesn't satisfy me...what I would give for UNDERSTANDING!

Answer: All that has to be given for understanding is the belief that understanding is achieved by a person. In other words what has to be given (or given up) is the 'I' that believes that it is doing the understanding. Take the following line for example: 'I want understanding' and see what remains when the 'I' and the 'want' are dropped from this sentence.

To help the mind recognize its own limitations, here are some more words.

All questions and all answers are mind and they will not directly reveal THAT which is prior to the mind, but indirectly each and every thought testifies to the Presence that exists prior to the mind; they point to THAT, which expresses via – and appears AS – the mind. Compare the mind to the light from a lamp, and compare THAT which is prior to the mind to electricity. The electricity expresses AS the light but remains itself invisible. It is there prior to its expression as light and it remains – non-manifested – when the lamp is switched of. This 'Priorness' is the Unborn, Self Arising, Mystery of Being. The mind uses words like 'prior to the mind' but it can never go there. It can use the words 'unborn, formless and eternal' but what they point at remains a mystery to the mind. Just try to imagine something that exists prior to the mind; is this not again just mind? Try to imagine the formless. Can there be any idea as to how to describe it?

You ask how things can develop if there is no time and space. Let's go back to the metaphor of the dream. A dream does not have any weight, substance or dimension, yet within the dream, one can experience substance, as well as the dimensions of space and time. In the same way Awareness – or THAT in which everything appears – has no substance or dimension. Within the 'dream of manifestation' substance, time and space are present and seem to be real; as real as a starry sky in your dreams.

You also ask, 'Who created thought' but we do not have to see thought as created by a separate creator. Instead, it can be seen as one of the ways the Unborn appears to itself. In essence thought and the source of thought are one and the same, just as the form of a statue and the stone it is crafted from. The statue is not created by the stone, but an 'appearance' of the stone. When we see thoughts as created, we may conclude that there must be a separate creator/thinker or God. The mind will then come out with the next question: 'OK, God created thought, but who created God?' The mystery we call 'God' or 'Source' is the Uncaused First Cause. This is not something the mind can grasp. An intuitive leap may reveal that the Source of all, including thought, is the Timeless One. There cannot be anything before the Timeless Source, as all before and after are again of the time dimension.

Thoughts are of the mind and our language talks about the mind as if it were a thing. However, mind is not a thing; it is the thinking process itself. Intuition may show that something had to be present before the words that make up thoughts could be acquired. It may also be recognized that the mind-stream appears TO something. Something (although it is not a 'some-thing' but rather a 'no-thing') which already IS before IT expresses via the mind as the words 'I AM.' IT is That What IS; the Original Face, peaking out of no-thing-ness. This intuitive leap may produce an 'Aha!... or laughter perhaps....

∞ ∞ ∞

Quick now, here, now, always –
A condition of complete simplicity
(Costing not less than everything)
And all shall be well and
All manner of thing shall be well
When the tongues of flames are in-folded
Into the crowned knot of fire
And the fire and the rose are one.

From: 'The Four Quartets' by T. S. Eliot

34. Science and the theory of evolution

Question: Hello from Albuquerque, New Mexico U.S.A. 'Awakening to the Dream' is the most fascinating book I've read. Advaita Vedanta is new to me, and it is unlike anything I have come across. My question is this:

The current scientific view of the manifested world is that there was a 'Big Bang' billons of years ago and evolution formed humans with consciousness or self-awareness. From what I understand, Awareness 'creates the manifested'. In other word, the falling tree in the forest doesn't make a sound if no one is there to hear it. So how could evolution take place to form 'aware creatures' if at one time, according to evolution, humans didn't exist on the planet?

Answer: As you say, the scientific view is of a 'Big Bang' followed by evolution, eventually leading to conscious beings. The Advaita view is the reverse: Consciousness/Awareness is primary. It is not dependent on anything, but expresses AS everything. In other words, the whole universe appears in IT. Science sees dead matter evolving into intelligent life, while to Advaita there is only IT appearing AS this whole manifestation.

Question: If all there is is this, it must have always been this, with no beginning or end?

Answer: Yes. Here is a quote from an answer in newsletter number 14:

When we perceive a universe with time and space, we also perceive cause and effect. When there is cause and effect there must be a first cause. This first cause must itself be uncaused; otherwise it would not be the first cause. It therefore has no beginning. If it has no beginning it has no end and qualifications such as before and after, or front and back, cannot apply to it. Without these criteria it is outside of – or prior to – the dimensions of space and time.

Question: However, science and the theory of evolution have some pretty convincing evidence, like fossils. Science tells us that our sun will eventually consume all of its fuel along with the Earth, and that would be the end of the dream...wouldn't it?

Answer: Perhaps. It is one way of looking at it. However, according to Advaita, space and time are in the 'Dreamer/ Awareness.' Concepts like 'beginning/end' are of the space/time dimensions and do not apply to the Timeless One.

Another way of seeing this, is that this whole manifestation vibrates into Being right here, right now, complete with buried dinosaurs, crumbling ruins of old civilizations, dying stars, and other 'evidence' of the past; just as it does in a dream. Here is a quote from the book 'Awakening to the Dream':

In our dreams we may encounter age-old mountains, oceans, stars, and planets. There may be people and animals, cities and forests. We may experience days or even years passing by.

And another quote:

The Dream of Space and Time
The dreamer contains the dream and, at the same time,
occupies a relative position in the dream. Everything in
his dream, whether rocks or clouds, feelings or thoughts,
people or animals, is made of 'dream stuff,' and as the
dreamed character, he can say:
Like the shadow
I am
and
I am not. *

Now consider the possibility that the Self dreams up this manifestation in a similar way. Like the dreamer appearing in his own dream, we can say that the Creator appears in his manifestation while, at the same time, the manifestation appears in the Creator. Dreamlike, He manifests the whole cosmic drama out of Himself.

He is hidden in His manifestation, manifest in His
concealing.
He is outward and inward, near and far... **

The substance of this dreamed up 'reality' is Pure Awareness – the dream that stuff is made of. In this reality/dream the mind appears and superimposes on this undivided whole the illusion of separate objects and events by inventing boundaries in space and time.

Let me ask you a question. Where did the event of 'you' have its beginning? Was it at birth, at conception, or when your grandparents' grandparents met? No matter where you draw the line, it will be arbitrary and defines an artificial boundary. In the game of day-to-day living, these conceptual borders come in handy; but most of us have long forgotten that they are entirely conceptual.

Awareness is self-luminous and does not need to be aware of anything outside itself. In other words, Awareness is all there is. In the universal dream, just as in the dreams we have at night, there is the illusion of this and that, near and far, past and future, self and other, which creates the relative experiences of space and time, but space and time in and of themselves have no reality. The 'mind-generated objects' in this universe are temporal occurrences and only have size and form relative to each other. Ultimately, however, there are no distinct objects or events separated by space and time, nor does the dream have a fixed size or time span. The dream and the dreamer are one-and-the-same self-aware reality.

---

* 'The Love Poems of Rumi', edited by Deepak Chopra. Harmony Books ISBN 0609602438
** Doctrine of the Sufis by Muhammed Al-Kalabadhi, Arthur John Arberry (Translator) AMS Press; ISBN: 0404146376

35. How to stop thinking?

Question: I was just looking through the 'How to stop thinking' topic (in the ATTD forum at: http://www. awakeningtothedream.com/forum1/index.html)and the subject of 'distraction and being present' came up. Examining my moment to moment life shows that there are times of 'being here' and times of 'not being here' although the episodes of 'not being here' are just memories. It would seem that 'being here' has some intrinsic value. The times of 'not being here' appear to be moments lost in thoughts or memories, thus the apparent need to stop thinking.

I am no longer interested in stopping thinking as such; the presence or absence of thoughts seems to be of little importance. However, the states of presence vs distraction do interest me. Is it a problem to make a distinction between these states, is there a difference? Does the value judgment implied cause a problem? Should I just drop the state of mind that notices I was distracted, should I not make an effort to return or hold on to 'presence'?

Answer: No effort whatsoever is required. The 'key' is in seeing through the whole thing. It is a bit like bursting into laughter. If it happens it happens effortlessly; if it does not happen, no effort is going to make it happen. It is beyond the grasp of the person. This does not mean it is all hopeless, but it points to the realization that you are not the person, you are, THAT which is aware OF the person. In other words: the person is an object in Awareness, and so are all states including states of presence and absence.

Real Presence is not a state for a someone to be in, IT is That which Is. Since IT IS ALL THERE IS, IT cannot be reached. IT is like space, and the I that wants to reach IT is like an object in space trying to reach space. Only the realization that it is impossible to not be in space will put the object at ease; only the realization that there is nothing but Presence will dissolve the agitation of trying to be present.

Just as space has no location but is the container of all locations, Presence is not a state, but the container of all states. IT is not an experience, but the experiencing itself IT is like a lens that can point everywhere, but never directly to itself. IT is like a light beam, which cannot shine light on itself.. It IS the light. In the same way IT is what you truly are; too close to see as it is the seeing itself IT is the canvas on which all changes, all states, experiences, thoughts and feelings (or the absence of them) appear. IT is the Unchanging Presence behind and in all manifestations.

When the recognition of this Presence comes in, the identification shifts from the I-person-object to the Ultimate Subject. Please see through these words, as they may be misleading. They may seem to suggest, that something has to happen, but the realization shows that nothing has to happen for IT to be AS IT IS.

∾ ∾ ∾

When the 'I' thought - the primary thought - has been
assumed, then the succession of arising thoughts appears
to form a continuous solid entity called 'mind'. It's like a
propeller: when it's still, it's seen as two or three blades,
but when it's whirling around – the apparent succession
of thoughts – then it appears as an entity.

From: 'Already Awake' by Nathan Gill, Non-Duality Press
ISBN: 09547792-2-3

36. False lucidity

Question: Your book reminded me of experiences that I have had while trying to lucid dream where I thought I was lucid dreaming, yet I was actually just 'thinking' I was doing it. I don't know if there is a term for that so I will just call it 'false lucidity.'

The problem is that in a false lucidity, I am trying to convince myself that I am dreaming, and I could even agree 'yes, I am dreaming' but the shift hasn't occurred where I actually experience and know that I am dreaming.

So, with your book and in waking life, I could read the book and say 'yes, I never did exist as a separate entity and I am the Pure Awareness that all experience happens on,' but this feels more akin to a false lucidity experience where there isn't that 'aha!' and the knowing instead of just believing it to be true.

Answer: The idea that there should be an 'Aha!' is still a subtle conceptualizing. It is still an expectation about THAT what cannot be conceptualized. You see, it is not an experience as such; IT is the in-experience-able experiencing itself. IT is the Ultimate Subject and cannot be made into an object, very much like light, which can never shine upon itself. IT is THAT which sees the true and false lucidity, but remains itself unseen.

We can also compare IT to sight. Sight's existence is clear from objects seen, but sight itself can never be seen; it cannot be brought into focus, as it is the very focusing.

Although sight remains unseen, its effects are

undeniable. Hence there is no belief about sight's existence, but a firm conviction. The same is true for the Awareness You are; everything appears to, in and on IT.

You AS Awareness cannot be known, as IT is the very knowing. When that is clear the conviction will take hold. There may or may not be a difference to the experience, there may or may not be an 'Aha!' but it is all seen as content to the unknowable/knowing context You are.

As Ramana said 'Understanding is everything.'

∽ ∽ ∽

'It is ... very evident that I cannot know as an object that which I must presuppose to know any object ...'

Kant, 'Critique of Pure Reason'

37. False lucidity, part 2

Question: I conceptually understand what you are saying, but it didn't put the question to rest for me. In the dream analogy, whether the character knows he is dreaming or not does not change the fact that he never really was an independent dream character.

Now, if some other dream character tried to convince the first character that he was dreaming and that he is not just his dream body, but also everything in the dream, he may listen to him and 'accept' this knowledge. Try as he might, this knowledge is only a belief to him, because he has not become lucid in the dream. He is still a dream character who wants to believe that he is not just the limited character, but also everything in the dream.

Do you see the point I am trying to make? I don't want to believe, I want to know.

Answer: The paradox here is that the 'I' that wants to know is a temporal object in Awareness. This I/dream-object cannot comprehend/know the subject, much as an object in space cannot grasp space.

You want to 'know' the non-dual IT while this requires the dualistic position of knower/known. Say that this would be possible and that you would know IT; then what would know the 'knower' while the knower is 'doing' the knowing?

Please don't get hung up on a metaphor. It can only take you so far, and then it has to stop. All use of metaphor requires thought. In other words it is nothing but mind

AKA the thinking process. What is pointed at here with words/mind extends outside the mind. The mind is here in the same position as the object in space; it cannot 'grasp' THAT in which it appears. This is the horizon that the mind cannot look beyond and here an intuitive leap confirms that if thoughts appear, they appear to something that cannot be brought into focus, as it is THAT which does/is the focusing.

This Awareness is Self-Shining; no outside knower can know IT, and I have tried to point beyond the pointing with examples in my last mail to you. Here is one more: the magic eye pictures that first look like random colors can all of a sudden shift into a clear 3-D picture. Nothing has changed in the picture; it was always already so. Seeing the image in the picture does not come from reasoning, but rather from a relaxed gaze that has given up a specific focus.

Certainty about IT does not come from reasoning, just as swimming does not come from reading books, but from daring to trust the instructor, entering the water and applying what has been said. Or compare it to learning how to ride a bicycle, which comes from trusting and relaxing into your natural sense of balance. Reasoning and the exchange of words can be helpful in learning those skills, but if one really wants to swim, or ride a bicycle, the words have to be left behind.

IT is not some-thing to be known by someone. IT is the knowing that cannot be known. In essence you are that Knowing. See that this is already so, trust IT, relax and BE (not BE-come, but BE) free.

ᔮ ᔮ ᔮ

Liberation is not about picking up a new belief system or a new set of answers (for example, that 'All is One,' or that 'Consciousness is all there is,' or that 'there is no free will,' or that 'you create your own reality,' or that 'everything is perfect.'). Liberation is the aliveness beyond belief, the aliveness of awareness itself. Liberation is when all the answers, explanations and positions disappear, and you're left with the open mind of not knowing.

Joan Tollifson, http:// www/joantollifson.com

38. Understanding is everything

Question: You quoted Ramana: 'Understanding is everything.' This sounds to me as if understanding is a prerequisite for realization. Do I have to interpret this as a portal? If the 'me' is a dream figure, who has to make the effort to come to understanding? Or is understanding a divine gift; is it 'grace' that annihilates the illusion of a separate 'me' in the apparent seeker?

Answer: Understanding as used here is not a prerequisite but another pointer to – or label for – realization. When it's understood that there is no separate 'I' doing the understanding then there simply is understanding.

Often the word 'seeing' is used instead of under-standing. This 'seeing' simply sees, without the idea that there is an 'I' that is somehow doing the seeing. It is not limited to the sight of the eye, and when the eyes close, the closing of the eyes is seen.

In this seeing, the blood circulates, the breath comes and goes, the tides roll in and out, the rivers flow, the clouds drift by and the planets move around the sun. It is seen that all this appears to happen without a separate doer in charge.

Nothing has to be done for IT to be as IT IS. If anything has to be done at all, it is to verify this truth inside. Have a look and see if there is a you who is having this look. Confirm the living presence that allows the reading of these words and check if there is a separate entity that can be located as the 'owner/doer' of this livingness.

When the absence of a personal doer is seen/ understood – by no one – it is clear that there is no you having a life, no you having thoughts, no you making the decisions, and no you doing the living.

This 'realization' shows that there is no one to realize anything, and no one who has to wait for grace or the divine gift of understanding. It shows that all there is is This exactly AS IT IS; not as it shall be or become, but AS IT IS.

From here (not from 'then onwards') all is seen as the Body of the One and it is clear that it is truly life living life AS you and everything else.

೦೦ ೦೦ ೦೦

Plop, there it is!

Nothing else than that, which is empty of matter, fills all corners of the universe!

Mountains, rivers, the entire world, you and all, they manifest the body of the One.

~ Buddhist verse ~

39. I am not the doer

Question: I totally accept this idea that 'I am not the doer'. I see that 'All is Consciousness'. I accept that good/evil are part of the interaction of the polarity of opposites and appear in phenomenality.

Recently I found myself at my doctors telling him about a physical problem and I asked him for a certain chemical solution, a thing I've always hesitated to take. He agreed and said, 'You are such an active person you want things to be ok right now. This will boost you up.' And it did and I feel great now. I know that Ramesh and you et al say that even though one accepts who one is the body/mind still continues to behave badly at times.

Can you help me to see what was taking place here? I had no control over what was taking place and I could see it while it was happening. I do not like this situation. I project all these great ideas to others and I am a poor role model. Not at all a pleasant situation to even explain away to myself. It was too overpowering.

Answer: It is not so much that you are not the doer as that there is no independent 'you' to either be the doer or the non-doer. You see, when we say 'I am not the doer.' often one idea of what one is, is traded for another idea. Like; 'First I thought I was the doer, now I think I am not the doer.' In both cases the belief in being a separate person may still remain.

There is no 'independent you' that accepts, that sees or knows. There IS acceptance, seeing and knowing, but it is not done by you. The person, the ego, is not in control; it is an object in the Awareness-You-Are. This clumsy use of language may suggest that there is a 'you' that is being this Awareness, so here is a rephrase: There is only This – Being-Awareness, in which everything appears including the body/mind, including possible thoughts of volition, of doing it right or wrong, and including thoughts of a body/mind that does not behave as it should.

It is the normal natural functioning for the body/mind to want to turn away from discomfort and towards comfort. Even the wish to be more accepting and to be a good role model is all coming from this.

There is a line in a Grateful Dead song that says: 'Sometimes the light is all shining on me, other times I can barely see.' Now this seems to be the human condition, but prior to that idea, there is this unknowable knowing, that knows. It sees both, the shining of the light and the 'I who barely sees.'

Again, it is 'nature's way' to not like discomfort and to try to move to comfort, but there is no 'you' in there doing it right or wrong. No 'you' that is projecting the great ideas and no you to be a poor role model. What is clearly shown by the body/mind not acting as one wishes, is that there is no 'you' in charge here. If there was, would this you ever choose to think unhappy thoughts; would it ever choose to feel miserable?

In and through all this comes the invitation to relax. If nothing can be done (if there is no 'you' to do) it can be seen that nevertheless everything gets done. The body is ill, it seeks out a doctor, the mind is sad, it will spin itself dizzy to feel better, and then it just might see it is helpless. In seeing that, a letting go may follow, but again... This is not a prescription that 'you' have to follow.

Take a deep breath, relax, no one in charge, no one doing it right or wrong... and here IT is... The present of all-inclusive Presence.

∞ ∞ ∞

You are like a mirage in the desert, which the thirsty man thinks is water; but when he comes up to it he finds it is nothing. And where he thought it was, there he finds God.

Similarly, if you were to examine yourself, you would find it to be nothing, and instead you would find God.

From: A Moslem Saint of the Twentieth Century:
Shaikh Ahmad Al-'Alawi', by Martin Lings,
George Allen & Unwin Ltd, 1961

40. Being close to awakening

Question: 'I' have practised Zen for 30 years, with koans, and I feel like being close to awakening but... is there something that could be 'done' right now? Many, many thanks!

Answer: Paradoxically, all that can be done is seeing that nothing can or has to be done; just as nothing can or has to be done to get closer to space. The 'I' that feels it is close, is but an object in the Awareness-You-Are. This 'I' does not have an independent existence and, when there is feeling, seeing, understanding, then it can be seen by no one, that there is no 'I' doing the feeling, seeing or understanding.

Here is the greatest koan of all: Who or what sees/ knows the 'I' that thinks it does the seeing and knowing? What is still there when all thought ceases? What answer can be given without reverting to thought and concepts?

Look for the silent center where there is no one left to do the looking. Find awakening where there is no one left to find anything. Give up everything, including the one who should give up everything, as well as the one who wants to do something to bring about an awakening.

As Buddha said, 'The deed there is, but no doer thereof.' When the idea of an 'I' with volition and the power to do, is seen through as yet another piece of content in the Awareness-You-Are, the pathless path ends right here where You have always been.

＠ ＠ ＠

...to say 'I do' is altogether false, because there is nobody who does; all happens by itself, including the idea of being a doer.

Sri Nisargadatta Maharaj in 'I am That', Acorn Press, ©1998

41. I know

Question: Intellectually I know there is only non-duality; have had experiences of cosmic understanding, etc; but right now, am wondering about the apparent 'kundalini/pranic movement' which is seriously debilitating, i.e. tremendous heat in feet and legs; tremendous pranic popping and cracking in 6th chakra or head.

I can't find any info from anyone who has completed this pranic journey except Da Free John...aka Ananda...aka other spiritual designations. He says: 'This pranic movement has nothing to do with realization of non-duality... they are two different things'

I am a dedicated web searcher and nothing has produced anyone (non-existing entity) that will discuss this in a clarification. Yes, I know 'I' is only a centre of awareness – a field and not a being-as-such; yet the physical vehicle of linking (body) is experiencing something that needs information.

Thank you – sorry to be so wordy – but as you said so well in your book – IT can't be described so well.

Answer: As long as there is the belief that I KNOW, the Knowing-without-the-doer is not ac-know-ledged. There always, already, is simply KNOWING and no 'I' to do the knowing. The split between knower and known, as well as between intellectual and 'real' knowing, are in themselves concepts arising in – or known by – the Knowing You already and always are.

The body and the kundalini experience arise in the

Awareness-You-Are. They are nothing but temporal content in the Eternal Context. Let's pretend for a moment that there is a 'you,' then let the heat rise, invite the panic in and look at it directly. Make it even welcome, say 'OK, do your worst, devour me', then be silent... even for a moment and see.

Now, what can it actually do? Generate heat and make a feeling that gets labeled as panic? What is it when it is met without resistance? What can it achieve without mind/labels or story line? What can it accomplish when it is totally welcomed in silence?

It is all mind, and this mind has realized that it has no eternal and independent existence. It knows the non-dual concepts, and now it is using them to hold on for dear life. In a panic it spins a story that it 'knows' the truth of non-dual-All-ness, and it has found in this a small island in the Ocean of Infinity, where it tries to make its last stand. In spite of its best attempts, it sees the non-dual waves eating away at the last remnants of the conceptual beach, and meets it with panic.

Really, let it do its dance, then accept, surrender and trust. YOU are itself the ocean claiming this small island. The fighting and the seeking for a way out has not helped so turn around 180 degrees and meet it. Be consumed like the phoenix, and see that YOU are not exclusively the body/mind. You do not need to fear, you do not need help, you are Freedom itself, and all experiences, including these words, are only your own Self inviting 'little you' to trust, to let go, and to see that there is only Home.

ഛ ഛ ഛ

In the ocean of being
There is only one.

There was and there will be
Only one.

You are already fulfilled.
How can you be bound or free?
Wherever you go,
Be happy.

The Ashtavakra Gita (15-18), translated by Thomas Byrom,
Shambhala Publications, ISBN: 1570628971

42. This crazy see-saw.

Question: I know all you say about IT is true. More and more often, IT comes, and then the person is no more, there is only a space that is alive, aware and filled to the brim with the 'ten thousand things' and so much more. And then I am all of IT, and, at the same time, none of IT, nothing at all, just the void, just conscious being and a wonderfully indescribable joy.

But then IT goes, and, again, I am left a prisoner of the tight confines of my skin, with all that maddening, noisy talk inside my head, which I can no longer stand.

When IT is here, that is not a problem, because nothing is a problem, problems simply don't and couldn't possibly exist. But when IT goes, it's hell.

Is IT ever going to come to stay, or am I going to live in this crazy see-saw forever?

Answer: There seems to be the idea that IT is an experience to be had by some one. Further there seems to be a concept that declares part of experience IT, and another part NOT IT. Remember, everything is IT, or IT is every-thing and no-thing. Even the idea that something is IT and something else is the absence of IT, is IT, forever non-dual, One-Without-A-Second. IT does not come and go, as all coming and going appears in IT.

What you describe as the absence and presence of the person – the seesaw – are experiences. By their very nature they have a beginning and an ending, they come and go, but the experiencing neither comes nor goes; IT IS. It is THAT in which everything – everything and nothing

– appears. It is THAT, which knows the coming and going of the thoughts, and the appearing and disappearing of the person. It is THAT which is aware of the absence and presence of problems. IT knows without any problem the idea of problems, without confusion it can identify confusion, and without the slightest doubt it recognizes doubt when it arises.

Yesterday's experiences and thoughts are gone, but THAT to which they appeared is unmoved and fully present. Take your stand there and see the revolving door of experiences turn without identifying that movement as IT coming and going. Recognize the knowing space as the constant and unchanging background/source, which does not come and go, as IT IS what always IS.

∽ ∽ ∽

'Kye ho! Wonderful!
You may say "existence" but you can't grasp it!
You may say "nonexistence", but many things appear!
It is beyond the sky of "existence" and "nonexistence –
I know it but cannot point to it!'

*Tantric Buddhist Women's Song' (8th - 11th c)
translated by Miranda Shaw.

*From 'Women in Praise of the Sacred: 43 Centuries of Spiritual Poetry by Women,' edited and with introductions by Jane Hirschfield
Harper Perennial, 1996 ISBN: 0060925760

43. There is no separation.

Question: I'd like to take this opportunity to comment on how almost all questions put to you concern the difficulties of grokking (!) that there is no separation of the 'me' and the big IT.

Answer: Yes, most – if not all – questions I receive come from the sense of being a separate character. This phantom is mostly seen as a responsible agent with volition, able to manipulate its destiny in time and space.

Question: What do you think of the idea that a person's mind is both the object and the instrument of change as far as achieving awareness is concerned... is this perhaps a misconception?

Answer: Awareness is a word that points to the Presence-That-IS, not to something that has to be achieved. As for the person and her or his mind, I have to say once again that the person does not have an independent existence. There is only the One appearing AS the seeming person with a mind.

We talk/write about the mind here as if it is a thing, but when looked into no such thing can be found. There is only the present thought. Even a changed mind is still an idea, which is itself nothing but mind. All the mind can 'do' here is to recognize its natural limitations.

We can also see the mind as the thinking process, which functions in the pairs of opposites. As such it is not the right tool to comprehend the One Context in which it appears. It can be understood that prior-to-the-mind is not some-thing that can be grasped by the mind and that anything that can be grasped, is itself mind. In this recognition the mind/thinking process can be seen for what it is. Have a look and investigate who or what it is that sees the mind.

༄ ༄ ༄

The whole universe is shining as One,
Without any split or break, or separate parts.
The idea of 'Maya' is itself the great delusion;
Duality and non-duality are merely concepts of the
mind.

Dattatreya's Song of the Avadhut.
Atma Books, ISBN 0-914557-15-7

44. Perhaps we need a new language?

Question: Clearly the greatest challenge for all of us is to put into words – which necessitate the use of subject/object – these truths, which are essentially non-dualistic. Perhaps we need a new language?

Answer: Or perhaps we need a clear understanding of what language is. As you say, it requires subject/object. A 'language' that does not have this division is Silence. The language of words (whether spoken, written or thought) is a conceptual representation based on past experience, and not the actuality it aims to point out, describe, or understand.

We will never capture the smell of a rose in words, but when we understand the function of words they can lead us to a flowerbed. If language cannot capture the smell of a rose, how much more so does this apply to the One Source of which every appearance (including language and rose) is but an expression?

The 'answer' is not in the words one hears or reads, but in the Awareness of such hearing and reading. Whether 'we' read the Upanishads or a billboard, the Aware Presence that knows the reading right now, before it is conceptualized as 'I read,' is the true Mystery-I-AM.

ော ော ော

Silence is the language God speaks and everything else is a bad translation.

Thomas Keating, contemplative Christian monk and interfaith pioneer

45. This sense of self

Question: Greetings Leo. You say that nearly all questions come from the SENSE of being a separate character... which makes 'me' wonder if this sense of self is not just a function of the brain like all the other senses, and like the other senses, cannot exist separately or independently but only in relationship with the world. How could the sense of hearing or touch be said to exist all by themselves without something to feel or a sound to hear? So, why can't there be a fully functioning and accepted *liberated* sense of self?

Answer: The sense of self and taking oneself to be a separate character are not necessarily the same 'thing' although they do get mixed up and cause confusion. The point to see is that this sense of individuality is an object in the Awareness-You-Are. The confusion starts when we exclusively identify as the object; i.e. the separate character.

When you look at these words, are you then these words, or that which is aware of them? In the same way, when you are aware of the person, are you then the person or that which is aware of it? This way of looking at it might be helpful to see through the illusion of being the person/ body/mind, but it is of course just a conceptual approach. Here we still maintain the dualistic stance of the witness and the witnessed. In the end they are seen as just two hands of the One Witnessing-Single-Awareness. In this Awareness, the sense of individuality can arise and have its function in the play of life. Seen AS a function/activity of the One, it is already liberated and fully functional. It is just no longer taken as one's exclusive identity since the falseness of that concept has been seen through, not by any one, but by Awareness itself.

∽ ∽ ∽

11-12: The self-effulgent light which illumines the world ever shines. It is indeed the witness of the world, the Self of all, pure in form, the basis of all beings, whose nature is pure consciousness.

From the Katharudra Upanishad,
translated by Prof. A. A. Ramanathan

46. A free hand to the bullies

Question: 'The mind is its own place, and in itself can make a heaven of hell, a hell of heaven' – Milton (Paradise Lost)... Isn't there anything we can do as individuals to help make the world a better place? If not, doesn't that give a free hand to the bullies of the world to do as they please?

Answer: No, we cannot do anything as individuals. And if 'we' cannot do anything as individuals, neither can the apparent bullies. The individual is not the doer, but one of the One-Self's 'doings.' As such the Self appears AS the bullies and the Mother Theresas of this world. All doing and not doing is from, for and by the One. All roles are 'played' by the Self. IT is the tormentor as well as the tormented; IT is the one who bestows blessings as well as the one who receives them.

∾ ∾ ∾

Get rid forthwith of doership, your self-identification, that is, with the agent, a distorted vision of yourself which stops you from resting in your true nature, and by identification with which you, who are really pure consciousness and a manifestation of joy itself, experience samsara with all its birth, decay, death and suffering.

From: 'The Crest Jewel of Wisdom' by Sankara
translated by John Richards

47. Who knows?

Question: If there is no individual self then who or what recognizes all the marvelously harmonious synchronicities, who or what feels the natural ebb and flow of events. Who trusts it? Who or what has the perfect vision, who or what knows that it is constantly embraced by the Almighty, who or what awakens to the dream?

Answer: It is the One-Self appearing in the play AS an individual, just as a dreamer appears within her own dream. When the character in the dream awakens to the dream – as in a lucid dream – it is not truly the character that wakes up, but the dreamer herself. It is seen that the character is but one of the manifestations of the dreamer, just as everything else in the dream. IT is the One who recognizes the synchronicity, feels the ebb and flow, and sees the beauty. IT IS the Mystery expressing AS all these things.

The 'means' by which IT recognizes itself can be mistaken for an individual self. It is the same fascination by which one might totally forget oneself when watching a movie or reading a book, completely identifying with the actor or character, while forgetting that one is in fact the watcher/reader.

In seeing that there is only One, it can be said that IT trusts in itself as a Self Arising Mystery that brings forth and animates all; from the smallest particles to the outmost quasars, blazing at the edge of the observable universe. This Mystery also appears AS you and THAT

Mystery is what you are; it is not something to be known, but the very knowing itself.

Now, from this perspective, if the character is moved to do good and compassionate things, it will no longer be claimed as goodness done by a 'me'. Action is liberated as it is recognized as only and ever coming from the One-Self-You-Are.

∽ ∽ ∽

Self is what you are.
You are That Fathomlessness
in which experience and concepts appear.
Self is the Moment that has no coming or going.
It is the Heart, Atman, Emptiness.
It shines to itself, by itself, in itself.
Self is what gives breath to Life.
You need not search for It, It is Here.
You are That through which you would search.
You are what you are looking for!
And That is All it is.
Only Self is.

~ Papaji ~

48. Sadness and hopelessness

Question: There is knowing that I am not the body or mind. There is knowing that everything is consciousness. There is spaciousness at times and not at others and still there is knowing that everything is included, everything is It. But there has not been a shift – the falling in love with it which so many speak of – only intellectual understanding. The intellectual understanding knows that there is nothing to do, there is nowhere to go, that the shift will happen when it happens if it happens.

So I have come to a standstill – I can't find the point of anything. What is the use of reading the next book or going to a retreat or listening to tapes and feeling 'spaciousness'. It just comes and goes as it will. Most concepts have disappeared; God, reincarnation, spirituality, right and wrong, etc. and the identities that formed a 'me' are eroding – I don't feel anything hearing the National Anthem, I take no pride in my ancestry, feel apolitical – just so detached from everything and everyone. It scares me that the drive to know the truth has just died. There is such sadness and hopelessness.

Answer: Hopelessness is the unwelcome twin brother of hope. Wherever hope appears, the twin is not far behind. Hoping that one 'gets it', is the nice way of saying that one is afraid to not get it.

It is clear that you have read a lot, but perhaps one essential point has been missed. That point would be that all these words and concepts are in themselves barren, just as the word sugar is forever devoid of flavor.

All words about 'The Truth' are mere pointers and have no ultimate truth within them. The words that come up now do not presume to be able to convert you to a hopeful person, but they are trying to point to THAT which is aware of the person; including the hope and the hopelessness. They say: 'Never mind what we read, the mystery is in THAT which is aware OF the reading.'

You know, words about falling in love with this, and a shift to be made, are also just concepts. Actually there cannot be a shift from the experience of hopelessness to THAT which is no experience at all. All these words point from and to IT. The word 'IT', as used here, stands for the inexperienceable experiencing at the very core of Being, prior to all states, ideas and concepts.

There is no one apart from THIS to fall in love with it, but as long as that position is present why not use it? What I mean is this: Surrender everything; all knowledge, all fear, all hope, all desperation and all ideas about a shift that should occur. Make all pain and depression that does not want to leave welcome. Notice all possible resistance to this and make that welcome too.

With your knowledge of non-dual philosophy, you might say that there is no one who can do this, but if this is truly clear, then there can also be no one to be hopeless. The apparent path of knowledge (Jnana) has brought 'you' to the edge. Why not jump from this edge, empty-handed, into the abyss of the Unknown? Or, if this is not possible, why not see if devotion (Bhakti) is available? Make the ugly twin brother at home and say to the ONE, 'Do with me as Thou willeth' or 'Thy will be done.' All this without hope of falling in love, and above all, without despair that it will not happen.

Surrender the idea that IT is an experience, a shift, or anything known, to be had by someone who now does not have it. In and beyond all this is the Knowing-That-You-Are, which cannot be denied. This Knowing-Presence is your 'Original Face.' It is the Unknown prior to thought, yet IT expresses as the thought I Am. This is what you ARE; it is not what you will become, nor is it something you will fall in or out of love with, but what you are: WHAT IS.

Finally, if at all possible, forget all this, and – if you are blessed with a healthy pair of legs – take walks in nature or in town – eyes and ears wide open – and be willing to be amazed with ordinary Beingness. If the question comes 'What is the use of all this?' see who cares. Simply BE AS YOU ARE.

೧೨ ೧೨ ೧೨

Just wake up from an afternoon nap in a grass hut.
Drag a walking stick and let it bounce free and easy.
Lean on a rock and watch the clouds rise.
Listen to the pine saplings and hear the sound of waves.

When the forest is dense, no guests pass by.
When the roads are dangerous, they're only used for
gathering firewood.
The place is so pristine and cool,
How could it fail to quench my mind's furnace of cares?

From: 'Poems on Living in the Mountains' by Hsu Yun

49. I feel like a dog chasing its tail

Question: I thank you for your wonderful newsletter. The question in the last newsletter could have been written by me. It is very much where I'm up to. I have been feeling a great sadness and haven't been able to explain why.

I have just come back from India and now feel at a loss as to what to do next. I know very well that I don't DO anything but after years of being a seeker of truth I now have the intellectual understanding of what is. I also know a life is being lived through this body and that there is no individual me to do anything but instead of the peace and oneness, this body is feeling isolated from the rest of humanity. How do you live a normal everyday life with the knowing that life just happens?

My family does not understand and try to find reasons for the way I feel. How do you explain to people that are not interested in Advaita? Your answer helped me a little and I have already tried the walking in the fresh air bit but it's not helping much. This will pass I know, or not, as the case will be. I've had the advice 'talk to like-minded friends' but they are a bit thin on the ground. I hope you don't mind me sending this to you, but then it's only what I'm meant to do. I feel like a dog chasing its tail. I know and yet I know there is no me to know.

Answer: First I would advise you to make sure that there is no mental or physical reason for the way you feel. Perhaps you ascribe it to the seeking while it also could be a chemical imbalance in the system. Who knows what your travels have done to the body.

Now that that is out of the way, the following comes up. The problem from the non-dual perspective seems to be that there still is the conviction that there is a separate person. I say this because you write: 'I know very well that I don't DO anything' and 'I now have the intellectual understanding of what is.'

Could it be seen that it is not so much that 'you' are not the doer, but that there is no independent 'you' to BE the doer? Also when the idea that there is an 'I' that HAS the intellectual understanding is let go of, understanding remains. Have a good look at this. Where is the possessor of this intellectual understanding? And what would be the difference between intellectual and true understanding? Perhaps it is imagined that true understanding would generate some happiness for the suffering character, but could 'true understanding' not be the realization that this character does not have an independent existence? Could it not be that the belief in such a character IS the suffering?

You say that 'a life is being lived through this body' I am not so fond of this 'living through' concept and prefer to say that Life appears AS the body-mind; just like clay does not appears through the shapes it assumes, but AS those shapes. It is easier to see that the clay, and the form are one and the same clay when the word 'AS' is used. In the same way it is easier to see that Life IS the shapes and forms it assumes when we say, 'Life lives AS all its forms.'

You say, 'I know and yet I know there is no me to know.' There is no 'I' to know anything, there is just knowing. There is no 'it' that rains and no 'it' that is cold. There is no 'I' that lives and no 'I' that knows; the 'I' is a known object in the Awareness-You-Are.

Awareness sees the thoughts appear as bubbles in a glass of sparkling water, all by themselves without a thinker pushing the bubbles into existence. Awareness is presently aware of the reading of these words. Turn around; turn away from the words to THAT which is aware of the reading of these words. Do not expect to bring it into focus, as it IS the very focusing itself. THIS is the simple and open secret. Always present AS what you already and forever ARE.

ುಲ ುಲ ುಲ

I am ubiquitous, both as absence and as presence,
Since, as I,
I am neither present nor absent.
I can never be known as an object in mind,
For I am what is knowing, and even 'mind' is my
object.

From: 'Posthumous Pieces' by Wei Wu Wei

50. A real sense of being stuck

Question: Just like the person's questions the other day, I am experiencing depression and I think it is caused by the psychological reason of not feeling 'held'. No proper base (extended stay at B&B), no relationship and looking for a project to get my teeth into which should allow all the above to click into place.

But meanwhile, whilst trying to get clear on what next, the sense of not feeling 'held' is seriously undermining the move forward. There is a real sense of being stuck, with feelings of hopelessness and on and off depression. It feels like a 'Catch 22'

What is this holding? Is this more neurosis, that when seen dissolves? Ramana was happy sitting in a cave for many years, needing nothing and no one, other than a supply of food that was delivered to him.

What is being missed here; what needs to be seen for forward movement to be possible?

Answer: If you really want to go forward, then psychological counseling may be the ticket. If there is a willingness to simply be, then no going forward is required.

Surely you have noticed that happiness, which seemingly comes from achievements, also seemingly disappears. I say seemingly, as it does not really come or go; IT always IS. Happiness does not come from the achievement, but is unveiled by the temporary absence of striving in the moment of fulfillment. Happiness is then wrongly ascribed to the achieved object, goal or dream, while it is in fact 'our' True Nature shining unobstructed by the clouds of aspiration.

When the object/achievement loses its sparkle, as it always does, the restlessness returns and the happiness seems lost. In fact, this happiness – or True Nature – never gets lost, only obscured, just as the sun gets covered by a cloud without being affected by it.

When this is known, there is the option to either pursue new desires, or to stay with the Uncaused-Joy-You-Are. This latter option means letting the moment take care of the moment. It is a total willingness to forgo all rewards, to forgo the belief in forward movement – along with all ideas of a better life later on – and to be present AS Presence, to what ever arises AS Presence; even when IT appears as dull or painful. In this willingness the person who endures and suffers will dissolve, and so, paradoxically, the way in, is the way out. Here the mind may come in and see this acceptance as the latest 'trick' to get what it wants. If or when that happens, let that be welcomed too.

Once this is 'taken care of' projects and 'holding' may or may not occur, but whatever comes up will be recognized as IT.

The One appearing AS the story of Ramana, sitting happily in a cave, is the same One appearing as you NOW. There is no difference, only variation, on a single 'theme.' You are that single theme, and all striving is the game of denying this; each step to get there is the pretence of THIS not really being IT. This is the illusion; the game of hide and seek the Self plays with the Self.

Are 'you' ready to see through the game, to admit that all effort is leading 'you' seemingly away from the Presence-You-Are? If yes, the game is up, yet still free to unfold as it wants. All 'better-later-on', which is the same as the illusion of really being a separate person existing somewhere on a timeline, has to be sacrificed for THIS. Here there are no stepping-stones, no thoughts to hold on to, nor schemes that can 'make it right' for someone… only the Immense Silence YOU ARE.

∞ ∞ ∞

'No particular thought can be mind's natural state, only silence. Not the idea of silence, but silence itself. When the mind is in its natural state, it reverts to silence spontaneously after every experience, or, rather, every experience happens against the background of silence.'

Sri Nisargadatta Maharaj in 'I am That', Acorn Press, ©1998

51. The presence of being

Question: There is a simplicity that I hear in your words that lets me step out of the striving, driving 'follower' mode. I too want to disappear into that Presence of being. Thank you.

Answer: What a wonderful paradox. It so clearly points to the heart of the matter: the wish for the end of separation. In essence all desire is the desire for our own absence. Intuitively it is sensed that this absence will bring clarity and peace. Yet – and here is the paradox – the desire for the absence, is the illusion of separation itself in one of its more elegant disguises.

This 'I' or ego that wants to dissolve is illusory and therefore not a true obstacle to understanding; much as a cloud is not a true obstacle to the sun's presence. What is more, when we look into this, we will see that the cloud is generated by the sun's own heat. In the same way the 'I' that wants to disappear into the Presence of Being is itself a reflection/activity of this Presence.

This Presence is all there is, so there is nothing that can stand apart from it to disappear in it. It may seem so, just like the cloud seems to erase the sun, and independent waves seem to appear and disappear on the ocean. These waves are in fact nothing but an activity of the ocean. Ocean and waves are a single body of water. Likewise, the One and the many are the expression of a Single Light, or of 'One Taste' as the Tibetan Buddhists say.

The mind translates this Single Light into dualistic

concepts such as 'I' and the Presence of Being, the permanent and the temporal, or awareness and its content. Here the concept aAareness represents the Eternal Context (like space), and all that appears (including thoughts and feelings) is its content. In THIS the 'I' is one of the objects that comes and goes. You-As-Awareness see the 'I' as well as its longing to disappear into the Presence of Being.

You – as this Single Light – are This Presence of Being, and nothing can or has to be done to make this so. In other words, You (as a separate character) never really appeared, so there is no need – nor any one – to wait for its disappearance. All appearances are again nothing but that very Presence of Being, appearing to itself AS the illusion of someone separate longing for reunification.

Rest AS the Seeing, AS the One Context and know that all there is is THIS. You are THIS.

∞ ∞ ∞

All beings are from the very beginning the Buddha;
It is like ice and water:
Apart from water no ice can exist,
Outside sentient beings, where do we seek the Buddha?

Hakuin Zenji (Hakuin Ekaku), 1689-1796

52. How might one achieve it?

Question: My desire is to understand what it is to achieve enlightenment, IT IT IT!

What is the experience of enlightenment all about? How might one achieve it? It almost appears, from my point of view, that the main point of all of this is being masked, hinted at, and slightly revealed in a teasing sort of way.

I would like to hear about direct examples of experience, in excruciating detail. What is it like? How does it feel? How do you know you're enlightened? I'm reading a lot of work by Ramesh Balsekar (non-duality) and it always seems to be skirting the perimeter without being direct. It's like this is some great secret that, once you attain IT IT IT, nobody is willing to share.

I have felt on the verge of understanding for a while now, and have had a couple of experiences that I've noted on another post, and I am ready for this to happen. But it's not happening.

Answer: This question lies at the heart of all seeking. The problem with the question is that it has inbuilt assumptions such as:

* Enlightenment is an experience.
* Enlightenment is achievable.
* There are enlightened people.
* and if it was to be explained in clear terms I certainly would get it.

Enlightenment is not a formula and it cannot be explained or described. All explanations are mind. Mind operates in duality and mind cannot comprehend what is prior to the mind, nor can you think yourself beyond thought. If it cannot be described, the mind might think that it either does not exist or that it is something very complicated.

Not everything that cannot be described is automatically complex.

Here is a simple example. Empty space: We know it intimately as that in which everything appears, including the body/mind. Now if we would try to describe space we will find it impossible. It has no shape, size, color, flavor or even a location. Everything that has a location appears in it.

That which is aware of space is even subtler. It is there all along but cannot be pinned down in a formula. Like the sun, this Awareness is Self-Shining and like the sun it cannot shine upon itself, nevertheless its presence is clear.

When this is seen it is not seen by the person, the person is a temporal occurrence in this Awareness. Therefore it is never the person who 'gets' it.

Do not believe me or anyone else who tells you what enlightenment is or is not. Like the taste of a peach, it cannot be explained, not even in a hundred books. Words can point you to the peach tree, but they cannot tell you the taste. You have to taste for yourself. In this tasting both the taster and the tasted dissolve and there will be no one left to claim the prize of enlightenment.

∽ ∽ ∽ ∽

'It is right in your face.
This moment,
the whole thing is handed to you.'

Zen master Yuanwu (1063-1135)

53. The longing continues

Question: This character can relate totally to the two recent letters outlining the despair and depression when it is ultimately realized totally, at the intellectual level, that there is no one to achieve or realize anything – but the longing continues.

This character saw very clearly, thanks to J. Krishnamurti, many years ago that the 'I' or the 'me' is a fiction. There was excitement; I could not get my hands on enough books, or attend enough Satsangs. Now the absurdity of the whole exercise is seen, and it is indeed depressing even though it is realized that there is no one to be depressed – it is all mind activity, all thought.

How can an illusion dispel an illusion? At times the thought occurs that it might have been better to remain in blissful ignorance. Clearly, however, it is seen that as it now is could not possibly be otherwise.

Answer: As you say 'How can an illusion dispel an illusion?'

What happens if we replace this question with 'How can an illusion hold on to an illusion?'

And another question: Why would one want to dispel the illusion? Perhaps one hopes to gain from it, if only emotionally. When we look into this, it turns out to be the same illusion again. When this is acknowledged, the illusion is seen through.

Seeing through an illusion is sufficient. Seeing through a mirage of an oasis in the desert does not dispel it, but there will be no investment in the picture, and no belief that one can go there and drink the water. It is enough to know that the magician on stage does not really saw his assistant in half, and that the sun does not really move towards the horizon. This knowledge will not prevent us from enjoying the magician's show, nor will it destroy the beauty of a spectacular 'sunset.' Awakening TO the dream; the gift of lucid living.

Response: Thank you from the bottom of my heart for your reply.

Your simple, clear answer, with examples, is beautifully put. It was like being hit over the head with a Zen master's 'wake up stick' !!

The ego does not give up easily, does it? Its apparent activities range from obvious to subtle. It will always exist (?), but is seen through. When there are lapses back into mind stuff, it is simply noticed, and disappears accordingly. The silence is immense.

Again, in deepest gratitude.

Answer: Wonderful! It is a pleasure to see the penny drop.

To rest as Presence and to be open to the subtleties of this simplicity is a blessing. Paradoxically, when the longing for a 'big bang' subsides, it turns out to always be present... even in and as the smallest whisper. It is clear that the Sun of Awareness is always there, whether covered by clouds of doubt or shining from the brilliant sky of lucidity. As Bob Adamson pointed out; 'When we investigate where the cloud that covers the sun came from it is clear that it is caused by the sun's activity. It's the sun's warmth that has evaporated the water and caused the cloud. It will also be the activity of the sun that stirs up the wind and blows the cloud away again.'

Whether the ego will always be there, I really can't say. It is seen here as the natural functioning of the body/mind. There are some tendencies, preferences, an apparent disposition and so on. One could say that this is the ego, but since it is an object in the Awareness 'I Am', it is not believed to be my exclusive identity.

We could also say that the apparent ego is an activity of the One-Energy and as such it is not an ego at all, as all is IT appearing AS apparent diversity. It does not seem to matter much how it converts into concepts. The funny thing is that it is as 'true' to say that I am the Limitless Context in which the whole universe appears, as it is to say that there is no one there to be anything; just Pure Being. Whatever we say, it is all translation or – as the film title says – 'Lost in Translation'… And even that 'loss' is nothing but IT appearing AS such. There is no way to find or lose the Beingness we are, as it is All, expressing AS All.

ೲ ೲ ೲ

'There is not a single state which is not this vast state of Presence.

It is the site and home of everything.

So remain in this which cannot be constructed or taken apart.

Here it is not necessary to progress gradually or to purify anything.'

From: 'You Are the Eyes of the World' by Longchenpa
translated by Kennard Lipman and Merrill Peterson, ISBN 1-55939-140-5

54. Chasing realization

Question: Even as I write these words, a part of me knows that it is a fruitless exercise. My mind chases realization of the Self, whilst fully acknowledging, at least at an intellectual level, that it can never grasp THAT which it seeks, because it is already part of THAT which is seeking. Yet all the while, mind continues to process all that it has discovered *in spite of* the fact that it is patently obvious that it can never understand or experience the Self in just the same way that the eye cannot see itself. It is so weird! In any other field of endeavor, given the knowledge and logic available, the mind would immediately throw in the towel. For example, if I had carefully researched the efficacy of a given drug, and the data pointed in a certain direction, then that would be that and my mind would be satisfied. No further effort required. Mind satisfied! Yet the desire for freedom seems to know no bounds, and so I have to conclude that this desire, although it appears as ego or mind, must actually originate and draw its power from beyond mind. My life is fine. I have enough money, food, experiences etc. There is no feeling of a need to escape, or to obtain a more elevated existence, and still there is this desire, which won't fade away.

Now, if object cannot know subject, which stands to reason, it fascinates me (or this mind) that the universal Self creates this scenario in the first place. Perhaps it is just its nature...who knows. Most of the writers in the non-dual area say that realization is a-causal, but from the minds 'point of view, this is absurd, particularly if you read the personal accounts of many of the people in whom awakening has occurred. There appears to be a common pattern such as:

Burning desire, above all else, to realize Self
Single-minded approach
Long exhaustive search for true Self
Dawning of the realization that there is no separate self that can ever know Self
Giving up the search
Awakening occurs, but is experienced by no separate self

Some may be slightly different, but it would appear not many! I know this ego will never know self, and yet the mind still searches. Will this end at some point... perhaps naturally fall away?

It is as if there are two of me – one that goes on searching, and the other that has already thrown in the towel, knowing that it's a complete waste of time.

Answer: It is of course convenient to use the word 'I' when communicating, but it might be a good idea to have a critical look at what it represents. It may be that there is an absolute certainty that this 'I' is what you (exclusively) are. The mind may say that it knows the fallacy of this but, underneath, the firm conviction of the 'I' as one's true identity may continue.

This is not unusual since when asked, 'Who are you?' many answers may come to mind, but when asked IF you are, there is no hesitation. Even if one would hesitate to say, 'Yes! I am', he or she would still have to be, to be able to hesitate. This certainty of one's being cannot be denied and expresses as the thought 'I AM.'

Now let's see. The thought of food may bring water to the mouth, but the thought cannot still the hunger; the food thought is not the food in the same way that the I-thought is not the True Self. There is something prior to thought that expresses AS thought and all other manifestations. It expresses as perfume in the rose, as sweetness in sugar, and as the thought 'I AM' in the mind. Actually these words are already missing the point, as the thought 'I AM' and the mind are not separate. There is no mind to be found apart from thought. Thought is mind, mind is thought. But, to stick with the metaphor, 'Priorness' which expresses as the 'I' thought cannot be conceptualized, as each concept is its expression. The 'I AM' thought can be confusing in that it suggest that there is an 'I' that IS, but actually this 'I' cannot be found separate from Being itself. I is the AM. In other words, there is only Being and not someone who is this being.

You say 'it (the mind) is already part of THAT which is seeking.' Actually it is not a part (apart) of it, but it is fully IT expressing AS the mind. IT is the Awareness that knows the reading of these words. Words come and go on this 'screen' of Awareness. This Awareness is the light that illuminates all objects, from the biggest mountain to the subtlest of thoughts and feelings. It is the Knowing that forever remains unknown, but can be inferred from all that is known. Much as sight remains forever unseen but can be inferred from all that is seen. This sight/knowing is ungraspable and at the same time completely obvious. The mind, being an object in Awareness, cannot get a handle on Awareness. This inability usually gets interpreted as that it then must be something very difficult. However something as obvious and clear as space is also indescribable for the mind. We see it everywhere, yet it is invisible.

Space is present, yet we cannot say it has a location, while everything that has a location appears in it.

What I want to suggest here is that the mind sometimes is just not the right tool. This may be hard to accept for the mind, especially if there is an intellectual tendency in the character. I suspect that this is the meaning of the words in the Bible; 'It is harder for a rich man (rich in concepts) to enter heaven, than for a camel to pass through the eye of a needle.'

If we compare the mind to a set of binoculars we may have learned that distant things can be brought into clear focus; as such they improves our vision. On the other hand we find them to be an unpractical tool when looking at things very close by, and when we turn them to the expanse of the blue sky we will find that they limit rather then improve the view. The same is true for the mind. It has its practical use, but its limits should be recognized for it to be really a useful servant.

Often the erring mind can be 'spotted' when it approaches the absolute with 'why' questions. It says things like 'Why am I?' and 'Why does the Self play the game this way?' Even if 'why?' could be answered, the next 'why?' can – and often does – come up. If you want to pay attention to the 'why' questions then see how they seem to be never-ending and often flawed like: 'Why does light make things visible?' 'Why is water wet?' 'Why does the universal Self creates this scenario in the first place?' As you suggested: because it is the nature of Self to appear to itself as it does. Just as it is the nature of light to make things visible, and just as water IS its wetness. If questions persist then – if at all possible – only pay attention to questions like: 'Who am I?' 'What is it that lives?' 'What is Consciousness/awareness?'

To the mind, the statement that awakening is a-causal can indeed seem absurd, especially when your six points are taken into consideration. However Awakening is ultimately not caused because it reveals the ever-present nature of IT. Say that we are looking at a magic eye picture; the pictures that look like a swirl of patterns and colors without a discernible shape or form. We are told that there is a 3-D picture hiding in there somewhere. Now we can try and try without result. When we are ready to give up, a relaxed gaze, revealing the 'hidden' picture, may suddenly replace the staring. It is not by our doing that the object in the picture is present. It was there all along. Also, our effort did not bring the picture to light, but rather the giving up made it visible. For someone who does not see the picture, it might appear that the persistent effort of the 'seer' has brought something into being, while in fact nothing changed, but the perspective.

With awakening this is even more so, as the mind that seeks IS the perspective that apparently prevents clear seeing. The cloud of thought may seem to hide the Sun of Awareness, but in reality it never affects its presence. Awakening is however not a perspective. It is IT recognizing itself as ALL. IT is already and always ALL. IT is THAT in which time appears and can therefore not be reached via a process in time, much as a fish in the ocean cannot reach the ocean by swimming.

A dream seen from within a dream may not seem to be a dream at all. Things may happen in a certain way and nothing but awakening will reveal the dream to be a dream. When the dream ends, all strife and struggle in the dream to achieve something is recognized as having nothing to do with awakening. Within the dream, getting somewhere may seem an option, but outside the dream all attempts by the dream characters are seen as irrelevant to the natural occurring awakening.

Now, after all these words, let's simplify a bit: You are THAT which is aware of all thoughts, feelings, hearings, visions, or anything else. This includes the mind that seems to keep seeking in spite of claiming to know better. IT is THAT, which sees the apparent 'two of me.' All these appearances are temporal. Even silence, mystical experiences and deep insights, appear to, on and ultimately AS the Awareness You already Are. They come and go, but YOU are the Experiencing-That-IS, and THIS cannot be made into an experience. It is already so. Let the mind do its dance till it tires out. If possible, don't believe it, don't follow the thoughts outward, but trace them back to their source, where you will find that You are this Source. Forever present, as Uncaused Presence.

ဢ ဢ ဢ

You cannot know the knower, for you are the knower. The fact of knowing proves the knower. You need no other proof. The knower of the known is not knowable. Just like the light is known in colours only, so is the knower known in knowledge.

Sri Nisargadatta Maharaj in 'I am That', Acorn Press, ©1998

55. Obsessed with this search for truth

Question: I understand that I can't do anything to reach this 'non-duality' or enlightenment. But why can't I stop the desire for it? It really dominates my life and makes everything else unattractive. I'm obsessed with this search for truth and I don't really have another goal in my life, I try, but in the end I think nothing is so precious as knowing the truth. Can you give me some advice please?

Answer: From the book you understood that you can do nothing, but if read carefully it says that there is no independent you to do anything. There is a difference. In the scenario where you can do nothing, you still seem to have an independent existence and you are helpless. On the other hand, when it is clear that there is no separate character, there is no one to be bound or helpless.

All advice I can give is to pay attention to the mystery of Awareness itself and to where thoughts arise from. To see if there really is an independent 'I' to be found anywhere. Have a good look. Is there really an 'I' that does the understanding? Is there an 'I' that does the desiring, an 'I' that does the trying and an 'I' that has a life? Can this 'I' be found? What is it? Thoughts come up like bubbles in a glass of soda. Where is this 'I' that does the thinking? When observed carefully, is not even 'I think' a thought bubble that comes up and disappears again?

Non-duality points to the realization that all there is, is the One. This means that there is no 'I' living 'my' life, but only Life living AS me and everything else. The 'I thought' is the label the mind uses to point to this Mystery that lives AS you. It is itself not the Mystery, just as the word sugar is not the sweetness it points to.

As part of the play of life, there is identification with that 'I' thought, so that there comes a moment that it is believed to be all we are. In some characters comes the wish to be free of that, which then can turn into seeking. But whether life appears as being totally absorbed in the dream of individuality, as seeking, or as being done with seeking, it is always just Life/Being itself

IT is never away from itself and IT can never reach itself. The separate character has no independent existence, does in fact not really exist, and can therefore not know the truth.

Life can and does, however, recognize its own play. It sees through the dream of separation and says 'all there is, is THIS.' This Living Presence is what the mind points to with the label 'I AM.' THIS is the Mystery of Being. Not something to become or get later on, but what I-AM-You–Are already now.

ꕥ ꕥ ꕥ

Omitting to seek after God, and creation, and things similar to these, seek for Him from (out of) thyself, and learn who it is that absolutely appropriates (unto Himself) all things in thee, and says, 'My God, my mind, my understanding, my soul, my body.' And learn from whence are sorrow, and joy, and love, and hatred, and involuntary wakefulness, and involuntary drowsiness, and involuntary anger, and involuntary affection; and if you accurately investigate these (points), you will discover (God) Himself, unity and plurality, in thyself, according to that title, and that He finds the outlet (for Deity) to be from thyself.

Monoimus, an Arabic Gnostic, who lived somewhere between 150 and 210.

56. What do 'I' do when awakening has happened?

Question: A question that has been haunting me since I came across the subject of Enlightenment is: What do 'I' do when awakening has happened?

Intellectually I know that there has never been a 'me' living a life, that life just happened without any guidance from a captain (as Jan Kersschot calls it) within me.

And yet I wonder where all of this energy goes which I've been investing (up until now) in becoming better, making my life happier, more fulfilling... My fear and at the same time my longing is to sit still for quite a while...

Answer: Clear seeing is about seeing through the concept of there being a separate individual who has to make his or her life work. The very idea that there is a 'you' with a life, wanting to improve it and sit quietly is the disquietness.

The phrase 'I know intellectually' comes up often in this context and is quite misleading. It says, 'I know that "I" do not exist.' If that is understood then there cannot be an 'I' to know this, which means that there is just knowing. This knowing – or cognizing – gets re-cognized by the mind and translates as 'I know.' See that the 'I' in 'I know' is itself but a thought and realize that there is awareness of that thought, without a you 'doing awareness.' It just is.

Seeing that this 'I' is nothing but a thought object in the Awareness-You-are, makes it clear that this 'I' has never done anything. Everything is always the One. It has brought 'you' out of no-thing-ness. It beats the heart, it renews the cells, it spins the galaxies and is free from all this apparent activity like a mirror that is untouched by what it effortlessly reflects.

This One can be trusted. It does not need help from a non-existing separate entity to make IT work. Relax – if that is given – and what will be done will be done... just as it always has. Only it will not be done by a 'you' or 'me.' As the prayer says: 'Thy will be done...'

∽ ∽ ∽

Clarity is freedom.
I had tea yesterday with a great theologian,
and he asked me,
'What is your experience of God's will?'
I liked that question – for the distillation of thought
hones thought in others.
Clarity, I know, is freedom.
What is my experience of God's will?
Everyone is a traveller.
Most all need lodging, food, and clothes.

I let enter my mouth what will enrich me.
I wear what will make my eye content,
I sleep where I will,
wake with the strength
to deeply love
all my mind can hold.
What is God's will for a wing?
Every bird knows that.

St.Teresa of Avila in 'Love Poems From God: Twelve Sacred Voices from the East and West' by Daniel Ladinsky, ISBN: 0142196126

57. Is awareness the 'doer?'

Question: You say: 'Could it be seen that it is not so much that you are the doer, but there is no independent you to BE the doer?'

Awareness as Leo expresses that and awareness as Marianne hears.

Could one say Awareness is the 'doer?'

Answer: Some questions may yield an answer more easily when the answer is not expected to be 'either-or,' It could very well be that the answer is 'both-and/or-neither.'

Looking at your question with this in mind, we could say that Awareness, The One, IT, is the only doer. We could also say that it just IS. We could say that the sun gives light or we could say it IS light. We could say that all that happens is IT happening, or we could say IT is IT. IT, AS IT IS, is Presence, not going anywhere, but simply being present. As such nothing happens, IT just is.

All perceived happenings are seen from a relative position. When we look at the ocean we can say it moves as the waves on its surface, as the tides that roll in and out, and as the currents that move within its body. We could also say that the ocean as a whole does not move at all and remains where it is.

In the invisible mirror of Awareness, objects move in and out of existence, the mirror itself does not move at all. Like in a dream, a lot may be happening, yet nothing happens at all.

∾ ∾ ∾ ∾ ∾

Nothing to do or undo,
nothing to force,
nothing to want,
and nothing missing –
Emaho! Marvelous!
Everything happens by itself.

From: 'Free & Easy' By Venerable Lama Gendun Rinpoche

58. This body will die

Question: I've written a time or two before and you have kindly answered. I've also read your book along with about a thousand others. I've attempted to look and look and look and, at times, I think I've got 'it' – whatever 'it' is. Yet, the truth is that there still seems to be someone here, an individual, called Vince, who is breathing, thinking, eating, driving, feeling irritable, feeling happy, watching movies, and who will die. This body will die.

Answer: Something seems to keep pulling you back to this inquiry. Your logic makes sense within the confines of its own assumptions and yet it does not seem to put the questioning to rest. You see, you are looking with the mind in the mind and all that is found is more mind.

As you say 'the truth is that there still seems to be someone here.' It is indeed the truth that there seems to be someone here doing all the things mentioned above. But is there really someone doing it, or is it just happening? Don't decisions, happiness, irritation, eating and thinking all just arise? Now there is a thought appearing. The next thought is unknown until it comes along. After it comes and goes, a new thought may come up to claim the previous thought by saying 'I thought this and that.' But where is this thinker that produces the thoughts apart from thought itself? Can it be seen that thoughts just appear and disappear of their own accord, and that ascribing them to a thinker is just more thought?

Question: When referring to an individual 'I', the reference is to this body, without which we could not be having this conversation, no? It will die. When it dies, this experience will end, will it not?

Answer: Yes, this experience will end as will any other experience. Where is yesterday's experience now? And more interestingly, to what do these so-called experiences appear? What is aware of their coming and going? Look at what is looking. It is as transparent – and as fundamental – as space, and just as easily overlooked. To the mind this Space-Like-Awareness is as empty as space itself, yet when looked into, this ungraspable no-thing-ness turns out to be the true essence one is looking for and from.

When you say, 'it (the body) will die', what actually happens? The four elements, which make up this body, return to the four elements and nothing is lost. At some point the sense of being an individual appeared and now it will break up once more, only to rise again countless times, and in endless variation. This body's 'I' may dissolve when the body stops functioning or it can be seen through right now.

You say that an individual 'I' refers to the body, but is this always so? To some it represents a conscious centre within the body, an ego, or perhaps a soul. And is the body not already there before this individual 'I' sense gets mixed up with it?

Before the words 'I AM' and their meaning are learned, there is already Presence. In other words, prior to learning the words 'I AM', you already are. There cannot be a conceptual memory of this 'Original Face' as it does not live in the past. IT is the Presence that IS and lives AS the questioning character.

∽ ∽ ∽

That which is not expressed by speech,
but that by which speech is expressed:
know that to be God, not what people here adore.

That which is not thought by the mind,
but that by which the mind thinks:
know that to be God, not what people here adore.

That which is not seen by the eye,
but that by which the eye sees:
know that to be God, not what people here adore.

That which is not heard by the ear,
but that by which the ear hears:
know that to be God, not what people here adore.

That which is not breathed by the breath,
but that by which the breath breathes:
know that to be God, not what people here adore.

From: 'The Kena Upanishad', English version by Sanderson Beck

59. Can there be knowing without a body/mind?

Question: Is there a way to know this world, to have this conversation, without an individual sense of 'me' having it (thinking, typing, etc.) via this body?

Answer: Absolutely. In one sense the view from a certain body/vantage point is unique and dictated by the senses, yet it can be seen that there is no 'me' having this view. It can be seen – by no one – that everything, including typing, thinking, etc, are simply arising without a 'me' being the owner of the experiences or a 'me' that's pushing it all into existence.

IT may know itself in a certain way by appearing as a body/mind. This body/mind may have a sense of personal doership, but it is still only the One appearing to itself as this sense of individuality. It is IT being individuality, just as clay, whether fashioned into an angel or into a devil, is still clay. IT is the One-Animating-Energy. This energy vibrates in and out of the forms/patterns that appear and disappear; somewhat like a vortex in a stream. The vortex seems to be a 'thing' in the current and it may hold its place and shape for a long time, but all it is is the river 'vortexing.' If the vortex dissolves the water that was its life and 'body' is unaffected.

Question: Certainly, if you were flying somewhere and the plane was going to crash there would be a sense for you of 'I am going to die', yes?

Answer: Perhaps. Twice I was in a plane that got into trouble and both times there was no real fear. Possibly the situation resolved itself too quickly for such a response to develop, but even if the thought 'I'm going to die' should arise, it would just be what is happening. A healthy body will automatically respond to a threat, as this is its natural functioning.

Question: When you stub your toe it still hurts, doesn't it?

Answer: There will be a sensation that might be labeled as pain, perhaps a curse, some foot clutching, and some one-legged dancing. That is what happens, but it is also clear that there is neither a 'me' that does the stubbing, nor a 'me' that is hurting, nor a 'me' that is the owner of the toe. There simply is what is, without a 'me' being the proprietor of it all.

Question: Without this body and brain we couldn't even talk about the concept of Awareness could we? So, doesn't awareness require the body and brain?

Answer: Without this body, there would be no specific body/brain activities. However, Awareness does not require bodies and brains; Awareness expresses AS bodies/brains and everything else. Saying that Awareness depends on the forms it assumes is like saying that gold depends on an earring to be gold. Gold is gold and it is not dependent on any form it assumes; it is the ornaments that are dependent on the gold for their existence. In the same way, it would be more accurate to say that bodies are dependent on Awareness for their functioning. Perhaps

Awareness is not the right word for you. Try: being, life, intelligent energy, or IT. IT expresses as thoughts via brains, as perfume via a rose and as sweetness in honey.

Question: The direct experience here is that being aware comes as a result of the functioning of this body and brain – there are no memories or experiences of before this body and brain were born.

Answer: Yes, before this body and brain were born, there weren't 'this-body-and-brain' experiences, but that which now experiences AS this body and brain was/is fully present. It is not something the mind can grasp; it is THAT what brings forth the mind and all its experiences. IT is like electricity, and the body/brain is like a light bulb. The bulb will function for some time and it will wear out. This does not affect the electricity.

Question: So what if we are all just waves rising out of the ocean of awareness!? The wave still doesn't want to die, to hurt, to suffer and it doesn't matter at all if the wave can know it is a manifestation of the great ocean – its experience is still that of a wave that will disappear. So what is the use of any of this?

Answer: 'Use' is a concept for someone who wants something. It is for an apparent individual who is taking the body to be 'his' identity, whilst hoping for a pardon of its wrongly perceived death sentence. It is a relative position, only applicable within the boundaries of the drama of duality. Non-dual, concept-free, Beingness has no use. IT is uncaused joy without beginning or end. It is the Ultimate Context in which the ideas of use and uselessness are but two of ITS temporal manifestations; fleeting like a dream.

The idea that we are just waves is a case of mistaken identity. THAT which emerges AS identity is not a personal possession, but the One Mystery expressing as the thought 'I AM.' 'We' are not just waves, we are the ocean waving; YOU – appearing as Identity – are the ocean.

∾ ∾ ∾

All phenomena are like a dream,
an illusion, a bubble and a shadow,
Like dew and lightning.

~Buddha in the Diamond Sutra~

60. Slightly out of focus

Question: Thanks so much for your book. I was a seeker for a long time, but the way that you expressed the truth was just what I needed to hear to bring about an understanding of oneness that wasn't quite here before.

I've been very interested in dreams, lucid and non-lucid, for much of my life, so the connection that you made with dreams really made it for me. It was a feeling of 'oh, that's how it is... now everything makes 'sense.' Beautiful. So, there is much appreciation here for your book.

It seems like everyone goes through the door of 'nothing' to get to 'everything,' but for me it appears backwards, at least in this mind – par for the course here I guess. I really don't know much about 'nothing,' though I do understand that That, or God, or Nothing or whatever you want to call it, is what I am and is all that is. It almost feels as if I cheated my way into oneness, like I know that I'm That without having more than a glimpse of what That is. The question or accusation comes up: how can you be It when you don't even know what It is, you don't know anything about the Nothing or the Void? And yet, from this new perspective of oneness, I can see that this question or accusation doesn't hold water either since whether or not there is knowledge of Nothing here, It is still what Is here. (I realize that all of these 'I's don't truly reflect this understanding of oneness, but I don't know how to communicate spontaneously otherwise.) Thanks again Leo. If you have any comments on the above, I'd be very glad to hear them, or if you don't have time or feel a response, I understand.

Answer: The way the understanding is expressed in your mail is like a lens that sees the whole picture, while being slightly out of focus. It only needs a bit of rotation of the focus ring to make the picture crisp.

You see, there can be no knowledge of No-thing. The No-thing-ness-you-are is the Knowing that cannot be known, just as sight cannot be seen. Light cannot illuminate itself, as it IS the light. IT does not know itself; IT is the Knowing-Self.

When there is only Oneness, who could be there to cheat his way in or out of it? All there is is this One-Beingness, expressing as the grand illusion of diversity. This diversity is nothing but variations on the One-Theme; like ornaments that appear all different and yet are all made of the same gold.

There is only the One-Substance appearing AS everything. IT expresses AS the individual character, AS the mystery to which the words 'I AM' point. You are That knowing-unknown Mystery.

ↄ ↄ ↄ

Give up all questions except one: 'Who am I?'
After all, the only fact you are sure of is that you are.
The 'I am' is certain.
The 'I am this' is not.

~ Sri Nisargadatta Maharaj ~

61. Choicelessly aware

Question: Given that there is no 'I' as a doer, is there any room for the concept of choice such as choosing to be choicelessly aware?

Answer: Yes there is always room for everything. However, it does not require an 'I' for choice to arise, just like there is no 'I' to do the thinking or anything else. Thoughts arise freely, as do feelings and choices.

The Awareness-You-Are that knows the reading of these words, also knows the choices that come up. The 'I' that supposedly makes the choices cannot be found apart from thought and is consequently nothing but thought.

In a sense Awareness is always choiceless; it neither chooses nor or avoids what occurs to it. All – including choices – is registered as a clear mirror registers whatever appears in front of it. The apparent 'I' is but a reflection in the mirror You are.

ᘒ ᘒ ᘒ

The wild geese do not intend to cast their reflection. The water has no mind to receive their image.

Zenrin Kushu , a collection of Zen sayings/poems published in 1688

62. Some hard questions

Question: I have some hard questions for you, which I hope you can answer honestly.

Answer: Let's see what comes up. I never know the answer until it appears, just as it is impossible to know my next thought until it arises. This immediately raises the question as to whether it really is 'my' thought or just self-arising thought without a 'me' doing the thinking.

Question 1: It is obvious to any person who has a bit of an inner maturity that all there is is this energy which is enacting this cosmic scene. But what makes these 'Advaitins' think that what they are saying is a truth? Where is the surety/guarantee of what Ramesh says or what Tony says? They seem to be so sure in advocating what they say as 'The Final Truth' that I feel the very title is misleading. What makes you think what Yogananda/ Kabir/Nanak/Farid say about soul and past lives and reincarnation is not as true as what Advaitins say, that all there is is Consciousness and there is no question of an independent identity to exist and survive? Whom to believe: Osho or Ramesh? And Ramesh seems to deride Osho. Was Osho fake? I don't think so. No fake can come up with what he did. Whom to believe then?

Answer: What you label as 'Energy' is labeled 'Consciousness, IT, God, Self, Brahman, Pure Awareness' by others. No one can tell the truth and neither Ramesh nor Tony says that they do. The truth can be pointed at by silence and by words, by migrating birds, a flower or by tragedy and suffering, but IT cannot be captured in concepts. The Truth is simple and wonderful but cannot be grasped by the mind. Even calling IT Truth and simple and wonderful is saying too much.

Imagine someone who has never seen or tasted a peach. How would you ever be able to tell him the truth about the taste of a peach? It would become a difficult task full of metaphors and comparisons without ever being able to really tell him how it tastes. As soon as peaches are in season you buy one and offer it to the questioner. First he has to believe you that it is really a peach you offer and not – for example – a poisonous fruit, then he has to taste for himself. One bite will dissolve all questions.

Yogananda, Kabir, Nanak, Farid, Osho, Ramesh, Tony, me, you, are all as real – or as unreal – as anything else. It is all the One appearing AS these apparent characters. In the end it is not relevant who is wrong, right, fake or true, as all these appearances are nothing but modifications in the One Substance. You have to 'taste and see' for yourself.

Question 2: Then there are people like Meher Baba who go with the traditional theory of karma, reincarnation, balancing out karma after death, and have given elaborate accounts of what happens in life and after life. Was he a fake? I don't know. It doesn't look like it.

Answer: It is again IT, appearing AS Meher Baba. If this is what is attractive and believable for an apparent separate you, then go with it, but it seems you have been 'bitten by the bug', after which mere belief/theory will never satisfy you.

Question 3: How can one reconcile their approach with Advaitins who believe that the cosmic play is being enacted through different objects (including humans and animals) in which they have absolutely no say, and volition is not possible? On the one hand, people are asked to drop the ego, make an effort. On the other hand, they are told to submit, because nothing is in their hand anyway, and this false sense of a doer is in the way.

Answer: The way I put it is that there is only IT appearing AS everything. There are no people, animals and objects with their own existence. It all is the One Substance appearing AS apparent diversity; much like clay can be presented in and as a million different statues. Most of the 'statues' in this life are dazzled by the immense variety in appearances, gods and dogs, devils and angels, heroes and villains, animals and inanimate objects while 'others' will recognize the One Substance as the One and True Essence in all this apparent multiplicity.

There is no one to be a doer or a non-doer. All 'doing' is from IT, just variations in this One Substance; as a pattern in water is nothing but water. One of the patterns appearing in this One Substance is the idea of separation and volition. We can call it a 'false sense of doership' but it makes no difference, because calling it so is again an expression of IT. That's why it is said that 'what you are seeking you already are.' The seeking is simply IT appearing AS seeking.

> It remains unaffected,
> Though It takes the form of earth, air, water and fire.
> Though It takes all these forms,
> It remains always the same. [1]

Question 4: If all there is is Consciousness, then obviously there is nothing wrong with my leading the kind of life I am leading (to hell with being 'good' and all that jazz). Maybe you will say I don't have a choice in being who I am or what is being enacted through me.

Answer: What I am saying is not that you have no choice, but that there is no you leading 'his' life and no you to make choices. Life is living Life AS you. Apparent choices are made, but there is no choice maker.

This is not 'new Advaita.' The Buddha said a long time ago:

> *'The deed there is, but no doer thereof,*
> *Suffering exists, but no one who suffers.'*

Question 5: But let's say I am leading a 'heinous/licentious' life where I take advantage of others. Am 'I' still at the same level as Ramana? And if there is karma, am I supposed to pay for my karma and not Ramana? This seems ludicrous. Either I am responsible or I am not.

Answer: Again, there is no 'you' leading a life or being responsible. If 'you' commit a heinous act there might be consequences and one might call this karma. When the play is seen 'through' consequences can still arise, but they will not be seen as one's karma.

Question 6: Then who determines karma? The theory of karma and reincarnation cannot be dismissed so lightly as they have been endorsed by many 'awakened' people in the past and the present, and they shouldn't be dismissed as being in error just because there is a new 'breed' of Advaitins who dismiss everything as a dream. Am I making sense at all?

Answer: The dismissal of these concepts is not new. For now let's pretend that time and history are both real. From this vantage point in time we can see that all great religions share the insight that God/IT, is omnipotent, omniscient, omnipresent. This leaves no room for anything else. Everything is IT.

All is Brahman and 'You Are That' is not a concept that recently came up. The Ashtavakra Gita, the Avadhut Gita, the Upanishads – to name but a few – are ancient scriptures, which point to the same inexpressible truth, pointed at by Tony, Ramesh and by Ramana when he said:

> *There is neither creation nor destruction,*
> *Neither destiny nor free will,*
> *Neither path nor achievement.*

And last but not least an 'ancient' quote from the Avadhut Gita:

> *I've told you all that constitutes the very core of Truth;*
> *There is no you, no me, no superior being, no disciple,*
> *and no Guru.* [2]

[1/2] Dattatreya's 'Song of the Avadhut', Atma Books
ISBN 0-914557-15-7

63. On having a distinctively troublesome mind

Question: I have to say that I really enjoyed your book – it was without doubt one of the best (if not the best) book that I have read regarding the way this actually is. I also recently went to see your friend Tony Parsons in Dublin which was a very interesting experience.

My problem still remains though that I seem to have a distinctively troublesome mind – at times I wonder if I am going insane. I feel total guilty for the extremely dark feelings, thoughts and urges which plague me. I feel like I'm in the middle of the worst nightmare ever!!!!!

Answer: If your condition is not caused by an imbalance in the system – and you have confirmed this via a health professional – then the following might be considered: When we read the above sentence it is full of 'I' and 'me.' If this 'I' is the one with all the different problems, then we should look into this 'I' concept. Who is this 'I' who has a troublesome mind, and who or what is this 'I' that is going insane and feeling guilty? Surely you have heard these questions before, now it might be the time to answer them truthfully.

Question: A few years ago I had what I call a kundalini awakening which nearly fried me both mentally and physically. The result of this is that now any time there is even a bit of a clear seeing for 'this as it is' my whole body feels like it's going to explode with the intense pressure from this energy.

Answer: What happens if it is welcomed? What if there is the willingness to totally explode? Invite it in and see what happens. I guarantee you that no one will have to scrape your body from the walls and ceiling.

Question: I'm lost beyond belief and wish I was dead. In one way I think I am so close to seeing this for what it is (if you can be close) yet at the same time feel like I am a million miles away. These thoughts of the darkest perversion are what truly crucify me. I just can't see how there could be any way out of this.

Answer: The bad news here is that there is no way out of it. The good news is that there is no one in this who has to get out. It may sound cryptic, but it simply means that there is no separate 'I.' All there is is One-Life expressing AS all possible options. One of its expressions is the sense of being an 'I' with a life. There is no 'I' to be the owner of a life. This sense of being an 'I' is LIFE itself appearing AS such an idea.

Question: It's funny in one way because I am a pretty popular person who gets on with everyone. I know in one way that I know this 'as it is' so well – I work quite uniquely as an audio-visual artist at times capturing the subtle essence of Presence which has always been totally familiar to me even from a young age. This was what was so pronounced after the kundalini awakening as everything seemed like it did when I was very very young. There was total awe for the beauty present in everything as it is. This is always the case when I seem to loose myself from worrying thoughts – a total wonder for life as it is. In Awakening is this child-like wonder how things constantly appear? I would thoroughly appreciate any help you can give me!!!! Thank you for taking the time to read this email!!

Answer: The beauty, the sense of awe, the wonder, as well as the pain, the agony, and the dark thoughts, are experiences appearing in and on the Awareness-You-Are. This Primal Unconditioned Awareness expresses AS everything. It expresses as the thought 'I AM.' IT is the Identity–That-Is -the 'I AM' of everything – and it is what you truly are. It is the One and Only Doer and Knower. There is no little 'you' that can do anything, all actions, thoughts, feelings are from and by this One Energy. Without it, the body would be dead meat.

When this is looked into, it will become clear that there is no thinker apart from thought; that this thinker is itself nothing but a self-arising thought. The same is true for feelings and actions. See through this dance and recognize that there is no seer, just seeing. The Centre cannot be approached; IT is the clear emptiness YOU ARE. All appearances are the content of this Centre or Eternal Context. The rest, such as ideas, thoughts, feelings, bodies, stars, monsters, trees and so on, is fleeting content. Know that You already and always are the Unknowable Knowing Context and be at ease.

‎ᕤ‎ᕤ‎ᕤ

I only am as all beings,
I only exist as all appearances.
I am only experienced as all sentience,
I am only cognized as all knowing.
Only visible as all that is seen,

Every concept is a concept of what I am.
All that seems to be is my being,
For what I am is not any thing.

'Posthumous Pieces', Wei Wu Wei
HKU Press, 1968, Part II, Chap. 32

64. There is nothing else

Question: I have a question. Can you help with this? There is pure Awareness and the objects in Awareness, right?

Answer: Yes, this is a way to speak about it, but in reality there is only Oneness/Mystery.

Here are two quotes from the book 'Awakening to the dream':

1: Zoom out, and Awareness and its content unify in a Self-luminous singularity about which nothing can be said or known for the simple reason that anything said or known is part-and-parcel of this singularity.

2: It is only because of the dualistic and linear nature of language that this text appears to split that which is essentially one into Pure Awareness and its content. In reality, there is no such duality.

In this dualistic description, Awareness stands for the permanent, while the appearances in Awareness represent the impermanent; but really they are the two sides of a single coin. However, to speak of two sides is still using two labels for one indefinable something. Perhaps it's a better metaphor to say that the height of the mountain is the depth of the valley.

Question: There is no creator only creation?

Answer: Yes. That's one way of putting it. Another way to see it is that the creator appears AS the creation: It is the same One.

Question: Deepak Chopra discusses how we create our lives by going into the gap and having an intention. What are your thoughts on this? If our life is being lived by pure Awareness (we are not living life but life is living us if you like) then as an object in that Awareness and also the Awareness itself, then what is the power to create in the gap by intention? I hope I make sense.

Answer: I am not sure what gap this is so the focus of the answer will be on intention and volition.

Let's say that as a child you hear someone play the piano, it grabs you in a powerful way and you're drawn to this instrument. Next you convince your parents to let you go to a teacher and she accepts you as a pupil. You turn out to be talented and learn to play with great skill. From this we can say that it was 'your' choice and 'your' skill and that it shows that if you really want to learn something you can, simply by putting in the will and the time.

Another story we can weave around this is that there was no 'you' that chose to hear that piano the first time, no 'you' that decided to be moved by that music; it just happened. From this came the talking about the piano to your parents, who did not choose to hear that story, but were nevertheless moved to find a teacher. In the presence of that teacher a talent (which you did not choose to have) unfolded and the hands and ears acquired the needed skills.

So if we come into contact with something that

resonates there might be a follow-up by looking into it and certain skills may blossom. Many will hear the piano, few will really play it. Others may hear a message of being able to 'create in the gap' and for some it may work. The One can appear as IT likes and such appearances may include apparent individuals, successful in creating 'their' lives through an act of will. However, this will not be done by the apparent individual; it always is the One appearing AS apparent successful characters.

As always, I repeat: There is no separate someone who can decide or have intention. All decisions, thoughts, actions, skills, are the One manifesting AS such qualities. As you said, there is only life living us. To be more precise: there are no 'us' being lived by life. There is only life. If we want to bring 'us' into the picture, then it is indeed Life living AS us.

∽ ∽ ∽

The beginning, the end, the manifest and the hidden.
The seer and the listener, all is Him,
He is in everything yet He is beyond,
there is nothing else, everything is Him;
abandon the duality of me and you,
see one, there aren't two at all,
understand this and disappear in it;
when you are not, then truly He is.

~ Hazrat Ali ~

65. Is this the same Advaita?

Question: I have your book. Now I am reading an article by Jan Van Delden. Do you think he is talking about the same Advaita that you teach?

Answer: No one can capture the Ultimate Subject into words. All words about IT are pointers and how they will be understood cannot be predicted. One may read all the Holy Scriptures without coming to clarity, or one may see a rose and suddenly be overwhelmed by the mystery that blooms AS the rose.

There is this inherent Knowing/Being appearing AS and IN all that is. This is the One-and-Only-True-Teacher. This teacher may appear as resonance with a person, with certain words, with music, with sights seen, or with absolute silence. Whatever it is, don't pay too much attention to that which seems to bring out this resonance, but pay attention to the resonance itself

If Jan's words are but an invitation to an intellectual exercise, they may never strike home. As such they are best forgotten. On the other hand, if they do resonate deeply, then the words can also be forgotten in favor of that resonance.

If it is 'time' for an awakening 'out of time' it will happen. In this awakening the 'you' that wants this awakening is surrendered spontaneously. The apparent separate character is seen through by no one, and it will be clear that Truth has never been hidden or revealed by anything. IT simply IS the Ever-Present-Presence expressing NOW as THAT Intelligence, which is silently aware of the reading of these words. You are THAT Aware-Silence and nothing can change that or make it so.

ᕙ ᕙ ᕙ

When you've seen beyond yourself
then you may find
peace of mind is waiting there
And the time will come
when you see we're all one
and life flows on within you and without you'.

Lennon & McCartney, 'Within You, Without You' (1968)

66. Why is there anything at all?

Question: First, let me say that I have no idea what is going on with reality, the world, or the minds in the world – including mine. I have been a 'seeker' for longer than I care to remember; I have gotten nowhere. I have a vague intellectual understanding of some of the concepts of Advaita, and I do mean vague! I 'know' (?) (vaguely, intellectually) that objects are concepts only, including myself. (Why can't I *really* know that?)

A couple of questions that have always bothered me are 'Why is there anything at all?' and, noting that there is something, 'Why isn't there everything?' How is it that the illusory things that we all seem to see, are the same for everyone? Why is there not an infinity of objects, including objects that no one actually sees in our consensus reality, e.g., green rabbits, soft rocks, a third sex, a different kind of water, more than 92 natural elements, etc.? How did we arrive at the world that we 'create' – and its agreed-upon objects – by perceiving it? If the Self that we all 'are' is what sees, thereby creating what 'we' see, why does It see what It does in fact see? It seems so limited, when I want It to be infinite.

It seems that the Self/world has somehow pulled itself up by Its bootstraps! If I am somehow a/the creator of my little world, who created me? And why? Is my anguish at not knowing just the way it is (tough!) because 'everyone' perceives it that way?

No doubt this seems like gibberish to you; it does to me, too. I hope you can shed some light on my ignorance.

Although I sense that this is not so as nothing happens. Awareness as Marianne plays at having a problem with this nothing happens.... what does Awareness as Leo say? Nothing?

Answer: As a long-time seeker you most likely have heard this before; 'The seeker is the sought.' You are looking from a finite seeker's perspective for an infinite experience. What if it turns out to be the exact opposite? What if the character is the Infinite having a finite experience? What if your true identity is the Infinite Identity expressing AS the 'finite I' having experiences?

When we look for what all experiences have in common, we will find that they all are finite; every single one has a beginning and an ending. Without such limits there would be no experience at all. It is the limitation of a cup or teapot that makes the experience of drinking tea possible. Or try to picture limitless organisms living forever. You will find it impossible to imagine. The limits of a body are necessary for there to be an organism, as well as birth and dying, which are the necessary borders wherein the experience of a living body appears. In other words, limitation is an essential ingredient in the game of existence.

Let's say that there were soft rocks, green rabbits and telepathic goldfish. Would they somehow be more amazing than what is right now? If such phenomena were part of our daily experience, we could again dismiss them as commonplace, limited expressions and ask for yet more variations on the theme of creation.

This reminds me of Alan Watts quoting G. K. Chesterton in his 'Book on the Taboo Against Knowing Who You Are.'

'It is one thing to be amazed at a gorgon or a griffin, creatures which do not exist; but it is quite another and much higher thing to be amazed at a rhinoceros or a giraffe, creatures which do exist and look as if they don't.'

The knowing you long for is itself the Knowing Mystery that cannot be known. It is what you ARE and that's why 'you' can't really know that. It is THAT which does the experiencing; more accurately (but still inadequately) it IS the inexperience-able experiencing.

Since this manifest universe is the expression of the One, it is not surprising that 'we' all more or less see the same reality. I say more or less, because from each perspective the view is mysteriously both unique and universal. When you think you are created and that you are the body/mind, then this limitation on True Identity is an illusion. Seen from the other side, the body/mind and the appearance of personhood is but a playful expression of the Uncreated One.

And yes, this One Presence seems to have pulled itself up by its own bootstraps from the abyss of absolute no-thing-ness. It is the First Uncaused Cause. When the obvious wonder of this is recognized, the not knowing is no longer painful but an exquisite amazement. Count yourself lucky to recognize your 'not knowing' and see the mystery of this.

Now, does it really matter whether IT appears as soft or hard rocks, as green or white rabbits or a consensus reality? It does not, for the forms it takes are irrelevant compared to the Presence of this Self-Existing Uncreated Mystery of Being.

∽ ∽ ∽

No-Mind

The flower invites the butterfly with no-mind;
The butterfly visits the flower with no-mind.
The flower opens, the butterfly comes;
The butterfly comes, the flower opens.
I don't know others,
Others don't know me.
By not-knowing we follow nature's course.

Zen Poetry by Zen Master Ryokan from 'Dewdrops on a Lotus Leaf',
translated by John Stevens

67. This sense of self

Question: I am wondering at the sense of self that accompanies the words 'I' or 'me'. I know from investigation that when this sense of self is closely examined it cannot be pinned down or grasped in any way, yet there seems to be something there. I know intellectually that the 'true' self is what is aware of the sense of self, but that doesn't make the feeling disappear. Does this sense of self vanish with 'Realization' or does it remain as an 'anchor'?

Answer: Does the sense of self really accompany the words 'I' and 'me, or is it the other way around? Is this undeniable, non-conceptual knowing that you are not already present before it gets translated into words like 'I', 'me' or 'I AM?' Don't they point to this 'knowing that knows that it is?' Please verify this and perhaps the concept of 'intellectual understanding' will drop away.

You use this concept when you say, 'I know intellectually that the "true" self is what is aware of the sense of self, but that doesn't make the feeling disappear.' There are two assumptions included in this statement. One is the dualistic idea that there is both true and intellectual understanding. The other assumption is that something has to disappear to facilitate the move from this assumed intellectual understanding to true understanding.

All this reasoning is mind looking within the mind for a solution to a non-existing problem. If there is a problem at all, then it is this idea that something has to happen for true understanding to be achieved by a separate someone. Such attempts can go on forever but they will never succeed, as this understanding is not an object to be acquired; it is what you always already are. It is the Witnessing Presence that you say you know intellectually. It is the One and as such there can be no other getting closer or moving away from this. The ac-know-ledgement of this does not depend on the pursuit of concepts, as this Knowing Presence is already fully present. Stop… and notice THAT what notices.

Like the hearing faculty, which is there independent of the occurrence of sound, the Presence that knows the appearance or non-appearance of a sense of self is fully present. The reading of these words, as well as the ideas and thoughts that get sparked by them, appear to and on this Presence, much as a film appears on a screen without affecting that screen in the least.

Habits, preferences and memories may be bundled together under the label of 'a personal self' but when this self is recognized as a relative position, which can appear or disappear on the 'screen' of Awareness, it no longer matters either way.

Many believe in the idea that this personal self should disappear, but this idea is itself part of the personal self structure. This self/object cannot remove itself from the screen it appears on.

If or when a personal sense of self comes into view then that is fine. It has no existence apart from the Awareness it appears on. Let it be… This too is an expression of the Undeniable-Beingness-You-Are.

❧ ❧ ❧

I am the light that is above them all.
I am the All.
The All came forth from me,
and the All returned to me.
Cleave a piece of wood: I am there.
Raise up a stone,
and you will find me there.

From: The Gospel of Thomas

68. Trying to explain the unexplainable

Question: The more I read the answers to the questions asked of you the more confusing Advaita sounds. Could it be that this is because you're trying to explain the unexplainable, or that there is no-thing to explain?

Answer: Yes, in truth there is nothing to explain. To the mind, however, this already is some sort of an explanation so it is faced with a paradox. Although it is clear that the unexplainable could not be explained, one can still repeatedly point to the obvious. This pointing points back to its source, while explaining would be from mind to mind and bear no fruit.

May 31 last year you wrote:

'I am grateful to you for your passing on of the wisdom of the Sages. As far as words are able to open our hearts and reconnect us to The Essence of Our True Oneness, they've helped me to understand that there is nothing to understand. THIS IS TRULY IT! Thanks.'

Now it seems that confusion is present. By the time this answer is read, most likely another frame of mind is present. Moods, thoughts, feelings and objects 'out there' all appear to What-You-Really-Are. This unchanging Essence is aware of all changes. It is the same Awareness that saw the words 'THIS IS TRULY IT!', and the more recent idea that Advaita is confusing, pass by.

It is this Awareness – and not the mind – that sees the

mind. It is this Aware Essence that is aware of all concepts that try to capture it. It is itself not something to understand, but the Source of and beyond all understanding. It is not something complex, but understanding in the everyday sense of 'grasping' something does not qualify for the job. IT is the essence of understanding and cannot be grasped. This is the mystery of One hand clapping. We could as easily say that IT is prior to and beyond all understanding, as that 'Understanding is everything.'

Look at these words... now turn around 180 degrees... forget the words... what is it that knows without confusion the suggestion of confusion? What knows the reading, the thoughts and the questions? What is aware of the mind trying to label this no-thing-ness at the very core of this moment?

To repeat your words: 'THIS IS TRULY IT!' Empty and Marvellous; the Unseen-Seer of all.

ல ல ல

Gone, Gone, Gone Beyond, Gone Completely Beyond, Awakened. So Be It!

The Buddha in the Heart Sutra

69. It happens when it happens

Question: This body/mind has been at this for three years. It appears that sometimes, 'I' am at the river's edge, but, for lack of a better way of phrasing it, the shift has not taken place. When you say, it happens when it happens, then there is a feeling of despair (thought of course), so that is how it is here!

Anyway thank you again for your interest and help. Would like to hear from you, if you have the time.

Answer: No need to despair on reading words like 'It happens when it happens.' All words are mere pointers to This As It Is.

The only 'shift' that needs to happen is to see that nothing has to happen for this to be as it is.

The Presence, that is aware of the reading of these words does not come or go. Everything appears in it, including the idea of a 'you' that is not 'there' yet. YOU are this Aware Context in which it all arises. The waiting for a shift is effortlessly seen by something that does not wait; IT simply is.

Turn around, away from the observed towards the observing. This observing cannot be an object to itself, just as light cannot shine upon itself. However, this doesn't prevent the light, or the Observing-Awareness, from shining forth.

YOU ARE this Self-Shining-Awareness to which these words appear. Now dive deeper and it will be clear that Awareness and its objects are one and the same Presence, just as object and form cannot be separated.

This Self-Arising, Self-Observing, Self-Shining Presence is all there is. IT appears to itself as apparent separate points of consciousness, but THAT which says 'I AM' in and as all these points, is the One-Self-You-Are.

No amount of waiting for an experience will make this come closer, as IT is not an experience, but the inexperience-able experiencing it self.

Waiting for a shift, not waiting for a shift, this text, the feelings in the body, they are all 'objects' appearing in and as the light of Presence-Awareness. The Self Originating Mystery that appears AS this Awareness will never be reached later on, by a non-existing separate character. YOU, expressing as such a character, are the Presence that IS.

໐໐ ໐໐ ໐໐

There is no need for you to become the Unborn.
The true Unborn has nothing to do with fundamental principles,
and it's beyond becoming or attaining. It's simply being as you are.

From: 'The Unborn : The life and teaching of Zen masterBankei' ,
ISBN 0-86547-595-4

70. Are awakenings happening now more than ever before?

Question: I've heard it said that awakenings seem to be happening more often now than in the past because there is a clarity now more than ever before. My question is this: Why would Oneness want to awaken to the game of separation in the first place? Isn't the whole point of apparent separation for Oneness to seek for itself? It seems to me Being went to great trouble to hide itself; or is this awakening simply inevitable on a larger scale? I would like to add how much I truly enjoy your book and the newsletters.

Answer: If we pretend that there once was a past then it is only logical that, since there are more people and more instant global communication options than before, that awakening should be happening now more than ever. I say 'seemingly' because there is only Presence and there never was a 'than ever.'

When we use the metaphor of a game to point to this manifestation, then we could indeed see it as a game of hide and seek, which is of course the same as the game of hide and find.

We may enjoy 'hiding' ourselves in dreams at night. As long as the dream is all fun and games we might like to continue to dream, but when dreams turn into nightmares we are glad for the wake-up option that's included in the 'dream game.'

After waking we can always fall asleep again and have new dreams... After the Self has found the Self, IT can rest outside time, until it wants to get lost again in a fresh dream/game.

Of course this is only a mythical pointing to THAT, which is beyond the reach of concepts, but as a pointer I like the hide and seek metaphor, in which the Self being alone (all-one) 'hides' in the apparent multiplicity of His manifestation. In this game Oneness 'forgets' itself in the game of 'two-ness' purely for the joy of getting lost and being found again. (A wonderful version of this hide and seek story is told by Alan Watts in his 'The Book on the Taboo Against Knowing Who You Are.')

Asking 'Why does the Self do this?' is a bit like asking 'Why is water wet?' Wetness is the nature of water and the way the Self appears is the nature of the Self.

Asking 'Why?' in a dream is itself part and parcel of that dream. All answers and explanations given within the dream are again nothing but the dream. On awakening the 'Why?' from within the dream loses it relevance. Dreams are just dreams and games are just games; there really is no 'Why?'

ᘛ ᘛ ᘛ

The Hindu model of the universe is a drama. The world is not made, it is acted. And behind every face – human, animal, plant, or mineral – there is the face, or non-face, of the central self, the atman, which is Brahman, the final reality that cannot be defined.

Alan Watts in his book 'The Way of Liberation', ISBN: 0834801817

71. From where do all those appearances arise?

Question: Here there seems to be an intellectual rather than a 'gut' understanding of the essentials that 'I am Awareness' and the ramifications of that concept, and of everything being Consciousness and its content. If it is a 'gut' understanding the 'answers to all questions' would arise spontaneously, as they appear to do for such 'reminders' as Leo, Nathan et al., because Consciousness acting as 'them' speaks from Oneness, and not from Consciousness pretending to forget!

However, in relation to the fact that all the 'people' reminding us of that fact say that everything (that we perceive) arises in Awareness: I have apparently allowed that, but 'no one' to my knowledge has said from where all those appearances arise. I have a feeling that the answer would be 'from Consciousness' or 'That is the Mystery', and that the mind's curiosity is always digging up questions wanting to 'know' things that maybe cannot be 'known'. The mind's curiosity is also Consciousness asking itself, because there is nothing else.

Any comments?

Answer: Since understanding cannot be an object to itself, just as sight cannot be its own object, I prefer to point out that there simply is understanding. No need to dualistically divide it into an intellectual and a gut understanding. There is in fact no separate entity doing the understanding; there is only the One expressing as understanding.

In response to your question, 'From where all those appearances arise?' the following comes up. Let's say that I answer 'It all comes from Source.' Then the question will just move upstream and ask where Source comes from. If we would then say something like 'From the Void.' we could again repeat the question. To me such an endless regression is an alarm bell, and it tells me that there is probably something wrong with the question.

Imbedded in this question is the assumption of cause and effect. Cause and effect are practical tools for reasoning, but they only apply on the relative level; they cannot be applied to the Ultimate Subject. This is Ultimate Subject is another name for the Uncaused Cause; it is Self-Originating and has been called 'the Unborn' by Zen master Bankei.

Clearly, the Uncaused cannot be explained in terms of cause and effect. Since the mind's activity depends on polarity it can never conceive of that which is prior to and beyond cause and effect. When this is clear, it is also clear that we will not get 'THE ANSWER' in a format that the mind can grasp. When reasoning recognizes its own restrictions, the need for a conceptual explanation drops away, and the questioning just dissipates.

We can call this falling away of the seeking, understanding or surrender. From this non-linear perspective, the Universe is no longer seen as caused by anything, but it is 'known' as the Presence-That-Is.

∞ ∞ ∞

'... it is absurd for the Evolutionist to complain that it is unthinkable for an admittedly unthinkable God to make everything out of nothing, and then pretend that it is more thinkable that nothing should turn itself into everything.'

~ G. K. Chesterton~

72. What do we really know, for sure?

Question: Maybe deep inside we doubt that non-dual stuff. Isn't it still very much against our everyday reality? If we convince others, then maybe there's something about it, and we may start to believe ourselves? What do we really know, for sure?

Answer: I know for sure that IT will always slip through the net of words, unless it wants to be caught. I know that THAT which escapes is the very knowing, that cannot be known, just as sight cannot be seen. And the deepest certainty is that I AM. Not that I am this or that, but AM; even to doubt this Beingness I have to be.

When retreating to the perspective of separation the 'everyday reality' seems indeed far removed from the non-dual perspective, but when the grip loosens, it flips the other way around. Then it makes perfect sense that it is sometimes called an open secret. Then (now) the dual perspective appears almost impossible and counter-intuitive. It seems a skilful fantasy that takes a lot of effort to maintain.

At this moment the whole thing collapses and even the crutches of duality and non-duality no longer support the phantom of the 'knower.' There is just the knowing mystery I AM.

ભ ભ ભ

Don't do a thing. Just rest.
For your separation from God
is the hardest work in the world.

From: 'Love Poems From God' by Hafiz, translated by Daniel Ladinsky

73. Why is this awareness restricted to one body/mind?

Question: There is no I. There is Awareness. Why is this Awareness restricted to this body and the input from the sense organs? There is awareness of the mind and its thought process. But this awareness is restricted to what the mind can perceive and imagine. Since the mind is brain based, is there awareness where there is no brain to perceive? Why is the awareness which is writing to you so restricted to one body and one mind?

Answer: This morning the sunlight passes through a crystal in front of my window, which projects various specks of light onto the walls. The reflections range from small white circles to stretched out rainbows glowing in various intensities.

The spots seem limited to their own boundaries, but are in fact not different from the single light that causes their appearance. Only because the light breaks up, this variety appears. When the crystal is removed they withdraw into their source.

When Consciousness breaks up into different 'light spots', it seems restricted to these spots. These 'spots' cannot go beyond their limits without fading away into the single light that projects them. There can, however, be a recognition that the 'spots of awareness' are identical with the Awareness that projects them. When that happens, it is also seen that this recognition actually does not originate in the limited character, but in the Source that appears AS the character.

Source plays as this manifestation and, to do this, limitations are needed to move the game along. Only by being limited in space and time can there be the illusion of location, of going from here to there, and from now to later on.

In a dream you can occupy a position relative to other dream characters and objects. You might agree or disagree with those dream characters and they even may surprise you with their actions, but they are all borrowing their existence from your 'dream stuff' and they all dissolve into nothing when the dream ends.

The drop cannot contain the ocean, but ocean and drop are the same water. Personal awareness cannot contain Awareness, but it can be recognized that it is all One Taste. So for the time being you appear as a being in time, but what you truly are is the Aware Centre from which this whole manifestation emanates.

໖໐ ໖໐ ໖໐

When the sun shines through crimson glass there appears to be a crimson sun, and when the sun shines through emerald glass there appears to be an emerald sun, yet is there but one sun which is neither crimson nor emerald.

And so it is with the one SELF shining through a myriad individual selves, which are as but the colored windows through which the sun of the SELF doth shine.

From: 'The Boy Who Saw True' by Cyril Scott
C.W. Daniel, ISBN: 085435493X

74. The seeking curse

Question: Thank you for the great book. Yours and Tony Parsons' books are the books to end all reading of books on this subject... You know, you've spoilt all the spiritual book-reading fun, ha ha!

I was wondering if you might be able to help or have any comment on the following dilemma...

It would appear that my mind or, rather, the mind is in a constant feedback loop. I understand and quite often notice that everything just arises in a space of awareness. But then the mind gets hold of it almost as soon as it happens and starts giving a running commentary or analysis on it, 'Oh, I wonder if this is awakening happening... Maybe it's just about to happen – that thing where everything just drops away and there's just This.'

The feedback loop continues as the mind catches the mind thinking about how this could be it, and then catches itself again thinking about how it has just caught itself thinking about how this could just be it. And while this is going on, there's an underlying expectation that this really could be IT!

The difficulty is that I know that I am powerless to seek or not seek this awakening thing. And I also know that this me seeking it and the frustration around that is just something else that arises in the Awareness which the me is looking for. Ultimately I feel I'm totally stuffed and sometimes wish I had never heard about any of this enlightenment stuff. This seeking is now like someone saying to you, 'Just try NOT thinking about a big pink elephant with green spots.'... You know what happens!

Answer: To begin with the end of the question: You are not powerless to seek or not seek, because there is no such entity as a 'you' to be powerless. There is only the One appearing as everything, including the mind, a possible sense of 'me-ness' and a feedback loop that cannot be stopped. Seeing that it cannot be stopped usually results in a search for solutions. However, it could also be seen as an invitation to find out whether there is really someone to stop it. If there is not, then there is no one in need of such a solution.

On investigation it may be discovered that the one bothered by this thought stream is itself a thought in that stream and the wish for this loop to stop may turn out to be the very loop itself. Any attempt to switch to not wishing it to stop, is still the same loop. It is working with the mind on the mind and as effective as fighting fire with gasoline.

So what to do? Perhaps it is possible to recognize that THAT which expresses as concepts in the mind, and as stars in the firmament, is not a concept that has to be gotten. IT is not something happening to you, but IT presently happens AS you. IT is what you are regardless of whatever thoughts are present.

Trying to get out of this loop is the loop. Is it perhaps possible to see through this double bind, just as you see that the instruction to not think about pink elephants is in fact a flawed instruction?

Although there is no one to do it, LET IT BE. With this 'letting be' and 'seeing through', the investment in the whole endeavour – to get a non existing me out of a non-existing problem – may slow down of its own accord; just as the 'investment' drops away when one recognizes a mirage as a mirage. In this recognition the mirage does not evaporate, but attempts to reach it or to fetch water from it will stop of their own accord. Something sees the loop, something sees the mirage. This unseen seeing IS out of the loop.

When the idea persists that there is someone who might understand this, then take it as a clear clue that the essential point is missed... by no one. This essential point is that there is no one doing or having such an understanding. When the falseness of the doer or possessor of understanding is seen then it is clear that under-standing simply is.

Confusion, feedback loops, or whatever else arises does so of its own accord and is nothing but temporary stuff appearing on the Awareness you are.

Everything is IT appearing to itself. The thought 'This is IT' or the thought 'This is not IT' are both IT appearing AS thought. There is no need to look for this Awareness as it is that which does the looking. That's why it is often said 'You are what you seek.' Light cannot shine upon itself it IS light, and the 'Knowing-that-knows-that-you-are' cannot be known BY a 'you' as it IS you. I AM (the knowing that knows) That I AM.

The mind may want to turn this description again into a prescription for 'getting it.' But really, there is nothing to get, nor anyone to get it. IT is Being THIS, and no one can learn or teach being. It is what you are. IT expresses as the mind in the thought 'I AM'. Or turn it around: This Beingness is what the thought I AM points to, in the same way that the word 'sweet' points to something the tongue knows, but is incapable of capturing into words. Is sweetness not simple and obvious? And is it not impossible to describe what sweetness is to someone who has not tasted it? The good news is that you are this Awareness, which can be pointed at by, but never captured, in mind/words/concepts.

Presently, there is awareness of the reading of these words. As soon as this is mentioned there is the recognition of this fact. This recognition is again seen in the Awareness you are, and so on. It can never be grasped as it is the very essence,which allows the grasping to arise. It is the finger tip that cannot touch itself. It is the Aware Presence That IS. It is that which knows the thoughts, but which itself is not a thought. It can not be turned towards or away from as IT is the empty centre around which everything turns.

Here now, presently, seeing the reading, seeing the thoughts that come up, including the idea of getting it or not getting it, this Simple-Everyday-Awareness is IT, regardless of the concepts that arise within it.

Start here, stay here. This Presence is IT. Nothing to reach, nothing to add, nothing to get and no one to get it. Just THIS Beingness appearing as everything and as you. IT is You, You are IT, and IT is IT.

ॐ ॐ ॐ

You imposed limits to your true nature of infinite being, then, you get displeased to be only a limited creature, then you begin spiritual practices to transcend these nonexistent limits. But if your practice itself implies the existence of these limits, how could they allow you to transcend them?

~ Ramana Maharshi ~

75. The full significance

Question: The last words of the book 'Ask the Awakened' by Wei Wu Wei is a quotation from Huang Po:

> *'Let me remind you*
> *That the perceived*
> *Cannot perceive.'*

(A more accurate translation from the same passage from Huang Po goes: 'You have been clearly told that the object seen does not see in its turn. Why put another head on yours…').

And Wei Wu Wei adds:

> *'If you should ever come to understand the full significance of this, will you not have understood everything that needs to be understood?'*

This full significance …What a jump! An abyss, is it not?

To put it briefly: I cannot feel you, Leo, as but an 'object' for 'Me' and devoid of perceiving, seeing and… answering…? Could 'you' help the motionless jump?

Answer: Here is a little twist on Huang Po's words:

> *Let me remind you*
> *That the perceiver*
> *Cannot be perceived.*

The very centre from which the perceiving emanates cannot be an object of perception, just as fire cannot burn itself. This centre cannot be known, it is itself the very Knowing. In its light all objects of perception are lit up. One of these objects is the perceived person. Another is thought or the mind.

This unknowable knowing is here right now, aware of the reading of these words and the thoughts that arise. It is the all-reflecting mirror, which remains itself beyond being reflected. It is the unheard listener, who 'hears' the thoughts as they tumble by. It is the ever still point to which all movement appears. It is the innermost innermost. It is the Presence that always already is the full significance.

∞ ∞ ∞

At the still point of the turning world. Neither flesh nor fleshless;

Neither from nor towards; at the still point, there the dance is,

But neither arrest nor movement. And do not call it fixity,

Where past and future are gathered. Neither movement from nor towards,

Neither ascent nor decline. Except for the point, the still point,

There would be no dance, and there is only the dance.

~ T. S. Eliot ~

76. Ending my spiritual search

Question: I read your book, and for the first time, things made sense. Thanks is too light a word for ending my 'spiritual search.' I subsequently purchased Tony Parsons' book and found it an excellent complement to your own.

The furious energy which has driven me relentlessly for the past five years of seeking has quietened, but some of the emotional baggage from my past still disturbs my efforts to just take things as they are.

There is now this sense of having so much time to just do ordinary things in daily life. But my life was so full of spiritual searching, that ordinary daily life had little time for anything else. Now suddenly, my days feel like big empty spaces with nothing in them.

I was watching a TV program this morning and it was showing several big-horn sheep grazing on the side of a mountain in Wyoming. They just ate grass for ten minutes or so, on the program, but the feeling of slowness and relaxation was immense! The pace of life in nature is so slow compared to the pace at which my mind has driven me for years. How does one slow down to the pace of nature? How does one relax after fifty-plus years of rushing around doing, thinking, solving problems, fixing things, learning things, improving things?

This issue is not 'spiritual' in nature necessarily, but simply the hyper-energies from youthful traumas and training that conditioned me to struggle and hurry as I grew up or conditioned me to perceive the world in certain ways. The mind, body and emotions are conditioned by the experiences of our past to twist our behavior to defend ourselves or scrap to survive in the 'real world'.

Answer: This is the last bit of confusion. It is all mind. If you are silent for just a moment – no thought – where is the past then? You see, the past – and an 'I' that is influenced by it – can only manifest in – and as – thought. I am not suggesting the trap in which there is a 'you' that has to work on silencing the mind, as this again is the same conditioning. It is the conditioning of mind-generated time and process in which 'I' will move from the restless conditioning to the restful new 'me.'

What is suggested here is to firmly say 'I am not just this mirage of a conditioned person, I am THAT in which this play appears.'

To label part of 'our' behavior conditioning is itself conditioning, as there actually is no individual to be conditioned, there is only THIS; Self-Arising Presence, manifest as everything/no-thing. This Presence includes and appears as an apparent character, conditioned to speak English, to believe in time, to identify with certain thought processes, and to call these processes 'me.'

You are this Presence.

Question: Most of these behaviors I find are performed or continued unconsciously. These 'mental and emotional programs', in their own way, encourage seeking or 'self-improvement behaviors' and emotional drives (which take one continuously into seeking behavior in the non-spiritual arena). Are these sorts of issues, in Advaita, of concern at all?

Answer: Let's compare it to a potter's wheel: it is heavy and keeps spinning because the foot of the potter kicks it at regular intervals. To start it, it needs some effort, but once it is going, its own weight/momentum requires only an occasional kick for it to continue. Even when the kicking is stopped it will spin on for quite some time. There is no need to try and put the brakes on, it will settle in neutral of its own accord. And when it does receive the occasional kick-start, there is still the knowing that the investment will subside, and that the wheel will assume its neutral position again.

Question: I found that, lacking a sense of peace and rightness in the spiritual arena, I could never be at peace in the material world. At peace finally in this dimension of my existence, I still possess similar drives and ego needs in my everyday world that continue to run.

Answer: Let them run. Once a mirage is recognized as a mirage, the image remains, but the investment will drop away by itself. No need to create a new investment, by insisting that now that it is recognized as an illusion it should become invisible.

Question: And even though I am noticing them, the restlessness and discomfort that drives them continues.

Answer: The 'I' that notices them and the restlessness and discomfort are all the same thing. There is no 'I' noticing them. There is just noticing. The 'I' in 'I think' and 'I do' is as real as the 'it' in 'it rains' and 'it is cold.'

Question: So I still feel at war with myself about slowing down and relaxing about life.

Answer: It will slow down by itself. The wish for IT to be different than it is, is the way it is, just as the wish for peace IS the restlessness itself. Accept everything; even the apparent inability to accept everything. It will show in exactly the right moment, that that there is no 'I' to be at war with 'me.' It will show that the 'you' who wants this peace as an experience is a phantom. It will show that 'you' will never have this peace, but that YOU ARE the Peace itself. Give Edwin and the body a break. Be nice to him, as you would treat a beloved child, and see in one moment of silence that there is no-thing to be done.

If the labeling of the mind stops for just a moment, it is enough to recognize that all conditioning, past, future, and the wishing for it to be different, is just a magic shadow show, with no more power than such shadows. You are the Clear Space of Awareness in which the dance appears, and like a mirror, you are never disturbed by what appears in it.

ɷ ɷ ɷ

For in and out, above, about, below,
'Tis nothing but a Magic Shadow Show,
Played in a Box whose Candle is the Sun,
Round which we Phantom,
Figures come and go.

From 'The Rubaiyat of Omar Khayyam'

77. Being present

Question: I can be present when I remember to be so...will it become natural at some time? Is there an unrecognised belief or story that keeps me from fully forever staying in that awareness even though the world goes on around me?

Do I need to dedicate time each day to go into Presence to strengthen this awareness as well as remember throughout the day?

Answer: The 'I' who wants to be present is a phantom. There is only Presence.

The word 'rock' points to an object, but is itself not a rock. In the same way the word 'I' points to something, which is not a word, and the invitation here, is to find out what this 'something' is. Is it not the undeniable Presence itself expressing AS the thought 'I AM?' This Presence is what is, and therefore it will not become natural for someone later on, but it is Timeless-Natural-Presence itself. It is best not to accept or reject this conclusion, but to have a good look by yourself for your SELF.

This One Presence, this SELF, is all there is. It appears AS everything, including the illusion of separation and the ensuing ideas that include a separate 'you' who can either remember or forget. You are not just this dream character who apparently remembers and forgets, but THAT which knows – and appears as – the remembering and forgetting right now.

When IT wants to meditate AS an apparent you, IT

will do so. Seeing that there is no separate 'you' to do anything will 'loosen the load' and this load will ultimately be recognized as totally non-existent.

See that there is no 'you' to do the remembering, the forgetting or the meditation. It all appears from Source; and Source is the only 'doer' in this whole manifestation. Every thought, action, feeling, every object or concept, arises spontaneously from Source like fragrance from a rose.

Source/IT does you, you do not do IT. This is already and always so. No need to remember or forget, just as you do not have to remember to be present while reading these words; and just as forgetting about being present does not erase the Presence that IS.

ༀ ༀ ༀ

All that is has me – universal creativity, pure and total presence – as its root.
How things appear is my being.
How things arise is my manifestation.
Sounds and words heard are my messages expressed in sounds and words.

From: 'You Are the Eyes of the World' by Longchenpa
Snow Lion, ISBN 1-55939-140-5

78. Mortality vs. immortality

Question: My query concerns the matter of mortality vs. immortality. If the Source of all is immortal, and generates Consciousness in which all phenomena arise, then physical existence is meaningless, is it not? And whether a person 'dies' or not is therefore of no importance. So when the appearances seem too overwhelming to cope with, why not escape from the illusion and automatically rejoin the void from which it all arises? Isn't that the ultimate Nirvana?

Answer: Source is itself Unborn and prior to mortal/immortal. IT is the 'meaning' of all things and the universal 'meaning' of all things is that they testify to Source from which they arise, just as all things seen testify to the presence of sight.

I put quotes around the word meaning because 'meaning' indicates that something has a relative value or that it is suggestive of something else. Through meaning we know what the word apple signifies. To some its import is food, to others it is the symbol of temptation, but an apple itself has no other meaning than being the apple it is. Meaning is a relative assessment, which cannot apply to the Absolute-All-There-Is. As the Absolute has nothing outside of it to point to, we can as easily say that IT is meaningless, as that IT/the Absolute is its own ultimate meaning and fulfillment.

Ultimately it does not matter whether a person lives or dies; it is part of the natural functioning. On the relative level of the dream, however, the death of someone may mean a lot of things to different people. So at the end of the day we cannot say much about it, as it does and does not matter at the same time.

The suicide option you refer to does of course happen, and for various apparent reasons, but there is no independent 'you' to decide on it, nor is there anyone to escape from the illusion. Believing that there is such a character is itself the illusion; such an illusion can as much escape an illusion as a character in a movie can step of the screen.

Question: P.S. While doing my NLP training it occurred to 'me' that NLP was substituting one experience, brain activity, for another, and I wanted to know the Truth itself, not just a happy dream. Or a happier dream than I (as an imagined individual) was currently indulging in.

Answer: Yes, this is part of what NLP does. It can be a great tool to maximize potential, to develop certain skills and to overcome limiting convictions.

The Ultimate or 'the Truth' on the other hand, is the unchanging background on –and in- which everything appears, including NLP, and different states such as happy/unhappy. IT is itself prior to, as well as beyond, any transient object or changing state. Therefore IT has also been called the 'Stateless State.'

Question: But since All is One, then the dream and the Truth are one also, are they not?

Answer: There is only Oneness, prior to the duality of one and two, or dream and truth.

Question: So there is no escape from the dream unless one awakens to it, as your book says. So there's no point in trying to attain Nirvana, because this IS Nirvana!

Answer: Awakening paradoxically shows that there is no one to escape or wake up; there is only IT appearing AS the dream. We can say that this insight is Nirvana, but it is and it is not, both and neither, beyond – and prior to – all such conceptualization.... And even the conceptualization is IT appearing as such.

> *Thou dost not vanish into Nirvana, nor does Nirvana abide in thee, for Nirvana transcends all duality of knowing and known, of being and non-being.*
>
> Lankavatara Sutra

To the mind this sounds complex, but this 'is/is not' is in itself as clear and simple as a landscape in a dream, or a reflection in a mirror.

∾ ∾ ∾

Seeker: If both dream and escape from dream are imaginings, what is the way out?

Nisargadatta Maharaj: There is no need of a way out! Don't you see that a way out is also part of the dream? All you have to do is to see the dream as dream.

Seeker: If I start the practice of dismissing everything as a dream, where will it lead me?

Nisargadatta Maharaj: Wherever it leads you, it will be a dream. The very idea of going beyond the dream is illusory.

Why go anywhere? Just realize that you are dreaming a dream you call the world, and stop looking for ways out. The dream is not your problem. Your problem is that you like one part of the dream and not another. When you have seen the dream as a dream, you have done all that needs be done.

Sri Nisargadatta Maharaj in 'I am That', Acorn Press, ©1998

79. Struggling with resistance

Question: I wondered, is it valuable to spend time in the presence of someone who is awake? My experience says yes ... and still our own work in facing our core issues – in surrendering – is essential as well. I have an opportunity to spend time in the presence of someone like this - and I am struggling with what seems to me as my ego's insanely strong resistance to this possibility. Any insights/comments?

Answer: There is an odd contradiction in looking for this kind of advice from apparent others. You have to assume that they know something you don't. Ask yourself, how would you know that they know? When someone writes out a long formula relating to quantum mechanics, how would you know what it means, unless you already have the ability to understand such a formula? The same holds true for what you seek. You already 'know' it, as it is what you truly are.

In the entire universe there is only one teacher. She may appear as another person, but she is not a person. This teacher manifests also as intuition – the inner tutor – and is available right now. There are no fixed rules as to how clarity will come about, but when it does, it is seen that the invitation to recognize one's True Nature is always fully present.

You seem to struggle with this option that has presented itself. I repeat 'you seem to struggle.' This comes from the idea that there is an independent character with volition, while all activity is in fact from the One. (Including the struggle, and the idea that there is a separate 'you' or ego.)

Whether you will go and spend time with this person, or whether you will not, may seem your choice, but it is the choice of the One only; this includes all thoughts that come up, all decisions that are made, and all feelings that arise. The apparent resisting ego is nothing but a spark from the One Fire. It has no power to resist of its own; all power is 'borrowed' from the One Fire it originates from. This One Fire is our True Nature and there is ultimately no difference between the fire and its sparks

Seeing that one is not the doer may be called surrender, but here it gets tricky, because there is no you doing this either. It is already and always so.

Now, if you find yourself getting on the road to be with someone who supposedly can point you to your own centre, then that is fine. It is not better or worse than staying at home and listening to the answer that comes from inside when you investigate what it is that is aware of reading these words right now.

I suggest that you forget about what you read, and ask what it is that knows the reading – right now – without having to say 'I read.' Turn the attention around, look for what it is that looks, and what it is that knows that you are. For example: We know to what the word water points, now see to what reality the concept 'I AM' points.

The answer comes from inside and from beyond the mind. It is not a formula, otherwise I would gladly write it out for you, but it is not complex either. It is most easily recognized in and as everyday awareness. This Awareness has never changed; IT is ever-present and effortlessly 'sees' everything appear and disappear without being touched by it, much as a mirror or a movie screen is untouched by its content. It sees the mind, the ego, and the whole universe, appear and disappear. Not much can be said about this Awareness except that it is clear, open and naturally present. Recognizing that this is not done by 'you' is Self recognizing Self. This re-cognition is a coming home to the place that was never left…. You Are That.

ⓥ ⓥ ⓥ

What exists in truth is the Self alone. The world, the individual soul, and God are appearances in it. Like silver in mother-of-pearl, these three appear at the same time, and disappear at the same time. The Self is that where there is absolutely no 'I' thought. That is called 'Silence'. The Self itself is the world; the Self itself is 'I'; the Self itself is God; all is Siva, the Self.

From: 'Who Am I' by Ramana Maharshi

80. Doing something or doing nothing

Question: I wonder about the difference between those who consider that meditation, stages of enlightenment etc. are of utmost importance, and those who are skeptical about that (Tony Parsons, Nathan Gill, you). It is as if you say, stop searching for what you are already now, and others say only a few are able, thanks to severe practice, to reach that goal. Both you and they name the same sages: Ramana Maharshi, Nisargadatta. Can you clarify this discrepancy?

Answer: There is no independent character who can choose to seek through effort, or who can decide to not make such an effort. Whatever happens is the way IT is, or the One appearing AS whatever appears. All action and all inaction come from the One. To quote from the Bhagavad Gita:

> *All works are being done by the Gunas (or the energy and power) of nature, but due to delusion of ego, people assume themselves to be the doer. (3.27)*

The Bhagavad-Gita, Copyright 1988 translated by Dr. Ramanand Prasad

Now Tony, Nathan and Leo may emphasize that practice feeds the illusion of an independent character who through its will may reach a future goal of enlightenment, but it is definitely not a new idea. Here is a quote from the sixth century. It comes from the 'Hsin-Hsin Ming' by Seng T'san, the third Zen patriarch.

Do not seek for the truth;
Only cease to cherish opinions.

To be sure, one can find plenty of quotes that encourage seeking and practice as well, but what if 'the doer' is a phantom? How could this phantom see through itself? How could a non-entity accomplish its own non existence? Is it not already non-existent, even when it is believed to exist?

Also, if practice could be the cause of clarity, then such clarity would be an effect. Since this clarity is non-dual it cannot be the half of the dualistic pair 'seeking and its result.' It is often said that IT is pure Presence. How could Presence be reached through time? It simply IS, and cannot be reached, much as space cannot be reached or left by the objects occurring in it. Nothing can be done by the illusory character to see this, because it is not this character that will see it. It is again the One appearing AS seeing.

ဢ ဢ ဢ

Since Buddhahood is not developed but occurs naturally,

You err in meditating and trying to achieve Buddhahood.

From: 'The Precious Treasury of the Way of Abiding' by Longchen Rabjam

81. What about this intellectual approach?

Question: I read these questions and answers always with much interest. But what about this intellectual approach? Much is written about Advaita and much more will be written about this. But perhaps it is about understanding only one or two sentences: The One is, and encompasses all, manifesting itself as everything.

Answer: The intellectual approach – or Jnana Yoga – is appropriate for those who are attracted to it. When the Jnana approach is taken to its ultimate conclusion it will end in surrender. Others are attracted to devotion and surrender, or Bhakti Yoga. When Bhakti is taken to its ultimate conclusion it will dissolve in understanding.

Ultimately, understanding and surrender both disappear into a Priorness, which cannot be touched by any concept or emotion.

This could indeed be realized from one sentence, one single word, or a 'roaring' silence. On the other hand, this inherent clarity could also be re-cognized after endless seeking and a million words.

At this point the whole mental construct around clarity falls apart. Words start to contradict each other and the mind loses its footing. Before and after no longer apply and instantly it is evident that neither devotion, nor an intellectual approach, can be instrumental to the presence of this all-pervading clarity.

From the seeking perspective it certainly seems that there is a process leading from confusion to clarity, but when the gateless gate is passed, it is seen that it was never really there, nor anyone to pass through it. Whether IT appears AS seeking or AS clarity, whether IT appears as a gate, or as someone passing through it, there always and only is Presence.

No-thing can lead to Presence, no-thing has caused the Uncaused, and no-thing ever obscured the clarity in which this whole manifestation appears.

So if there is any credit to be given for the clarity that IS, it neither goes to a single sentence nor to a library of books; all 'credit' goes to no-thing.

෨෨ ෨෨ ෨෨

Thirty spokes on a cartwheel go towards the hub that is the centre – but look, there is nothing at the centre and that is precisely why it works!

If you mould a cup, you have to make it hollow: it is the emptiness within it that makes it useful.

In a house or room, it is the empty spaces – the doors, the windows – that make it useable.

They all use what they are made of to do what they do, but without their nothingness they would be nothing.

'Tao Te Ching' (11) translated by Man-Ho Kwok, M. Palmer, and J. Ramsay.
ISBN: 1843336278

82. The central 'I' character

Question: Once again I would very much appreciate some help if you wouldn't mind! Basically it boils down to the fact that although I can see that thoughts, moods, emotions etc all arise without any instigator or personal doer, they do appear to arise for an 'I' that prefers some of these and not others. This for me appears to be the central 'I' character or individual personality.

Answer: Yes, as you say, 'Thoughts, moods, emotions etc, all arise without any instigator or personal doer.' The same holds true for the preferences and 'I character' you mention. This 'I' is nothing but the occurrence of a reference point within the field of Awareness. It is but another perceived 'object', just like moods, emotions thoughts and preferences.

Question: Is it literally true that there is no one there? If so it seems that that would be a shocking revelation unlike the suggestion by some of the 'no one home club' that it is a simple shift in perspective.

Answer: As there really is no individual doer, and the 'I' in 'I think.' is itself a thought, it can be said that there literally is no one there. On the other hand there is this undeniable Presence, expressing as the thought 'I AM'. This Presence is True Identity being you, me, everything, yet no-thing, and as such there is no 'I' being IT; only IT being 'I'.

The 'simple shift in perspective' is from the belief that there is someone doing the thinking, seeing and feeling, to the realization that there only IS thinking, seeing, and feeling. What, for example, needs to be done for thoughts to come up? Are they not Self arising? Do 'I' know 'my' next thought before it appears? Does the 'I thought' knows the thoughts, or are they simply known when present?

Question: How could one know for certain that this is the case anyway? The mind has an amazing ability to make us believe all sorts of incredible possibilities, so what's different about awakening that would rule this out as a possibility?

Answer: Thoughts, beliefs, and assumptions appear to and in 'something' which is not a thought, belief, or assumption. This is the Knowing that knows each thought as it appears. Even if we could find a way to proof this beyond doubt, the Knowing that knows this prove could not be known or proven, much as sight cannot be seen and hearing cannot be heard. IT is self-evident, its own proof and certainty. Like the sun, which cannot shine on itself, the Knowing Presence cannot be an object of knowing to itself. All we can say is: 'Look! What is it that knows the looking?'

Question: Finally I have to say that during any periods in my life where the train of thoughts seem to subside there is a lovely sense of aliveness which comes shining through – e.g. when waking up one morning a few years ago the world outside the window appeared to have a vibrant aliveness, unlike the usual murkiness when negative thoughts prevail.

This was like a haunting reminder of the childlike state of Presence which I had almost forgotten till that point – forgotten yet still somehow remembered would be more accurate if that makes any sense! When this Presence comes shining through everything feels so radically alive and wondrous. Is this comparable to awakening where there is little absorption in negativity? This is such a beautiful state where wishing for this, that and the other seems to evaporate!!

Any help you could give me would be much appreciated Leo! Thanks ever so much for taking the time to read this.

Answer: Thank you too; it is a great question and a beautiful conclusion. The only thing I have to add to this is that 'the Presence that comes shining through' is not really a state to be in. It can be called the Natural State or the Stateless State or Uncaused Joy. IT has no reason for being, but is the reason for all that is. IT is its own cause and its own fulfillment. IT is Pure Experiencing and the 'post mortem' attempts of the mind to introduce an 'I' doing this experiencing, an 'I' who has the joy, or who is in this state, is as useful as adding legs to a snake.

The mind, labeling the childlike state as preferable to thoughts that are seen as negative, can promote a fascination with certain mental and emotional states. It can take the attention on a wild ride, looking for all kinds of 'positive' experiences, overlooking the fact that ALL experiences and states of mind are but temporal occurrences in Ever Present, Primal, and Pure Awareness.

Now that these words are read, is there a thought going on, constantly repeating 'I read. I read'? Or does the actual reading have to be suspended to say this? When the thought of an 'I' doing the reading is not present, Presence nevertheless remains, unobstructed, unforced and fully aware of the reading.

Thoughts and experiences – whether labeled as negative or positive – may on the face of it make this Presence disappear, but in reality nothing can touch THIS; just as rain clouds cannot touch or extinguish the sun. From the 'I perspective' the sun gets obscured by the clouds, but from the 'sun perspective' the clouds are temporal objects being lit up in its rays. So whatever thoughts or states present themselves in the Light of Awareness, whatever clouds drift by, IT always shines unobstructed. IT is the Source of all, and presently IT is appearing in its own game AS you.

88. Being knowledge itself He does not understand 'to know Himself.' It is as difficult as the perception of the eye by itself.

89. Knowledge would be able to know itself if the mirror would be able to reflect its own image.

90. A knife would be able to pierce a thing that is beyond all quarters by moving towards it. But can it pierce itself?

91. The tip of the tongue is expert in tasting but can it taste itself?

92. But does its existence as an organ of tasting cease on that account? It is not so because tasting is immanent in it.

93. So the Atman, who is knowledge, existence and bliss, is self-evident. How can the word offer him that which is already his?

94. The Ultimate Substance does not prove or disprove itself with the help of any means of knowledge. It is self-evident, self-existent and beyond proof or disproof.

Sri Jnanadeva in the Amritanubhava

83. A state I yearn for

Question: Just stumbled across your website tonight and read the excerpt from the last chapter of your book. Nicely done. Your description of this enlightened state is done with simple elegance.

Have you personally experienced this state? It's a state I yearn for.

Answer: That enlightenment would be an experience or a state for someone to be in, constitutes the enlightenment myth. Enlightenment is not so much an experience for someone that it is freedom from being a someone. Yes there are wonderful experiences (peak experiences or mystical experiences) which often get confused with enlightenment. True enlightenment is already fully present, but as long as the mind thinks it's some kind of an experience, it gets overlooked.

Your true identity is the ultimate subject and it is effortlessly aware of everything. To this ultimate subject – to this witnessing presence – everything that appears is an object, including thoughts, the ego and the mind. Seen from this angle the mind appears in awareness. Shift the attention from the experience to the experiencing itself, from the seen (the mind) to the seeing and from the known to the knowing, and it will all be clear. Seeing can never be seen by the eye and this 'knowing' can never be an object to itself, which is the reason that it is – as so often said – beyond the mind.

I wish you the clarity you yearn for, but be careful, as

it will annihilate the 'you' that yearns for it.

∽ ∽ ∽

You wander from room to room,
Hunting for the diamond necklace,
That is already around your neck!

~ Rumi ~

84. The body is an illusion

Question: If the body is an illusion or Maya, why would an awakened person need to keep feeding it? Isn't that a form of ego addiction?

Answer: What if awakening reveals that the real illusion is the idea of separation and personhood? Wouldn't this make an 'enlightened person' an 'enlightened illusion'?

Imagine a stage magician, pulling a coin out of your ear. You know that it is an illusion. However, the illusion is not in the appearance of the coin, but in where it seems to come from. In the same way, the body illusion is not in the appearing of the body, but in identifying with it as that which you exclusively are.

Awakening shows that what you are is not confined to this body; nor are you just a person, or an individual soul. Awakening is the impersonal recognition of THAT which expresses AS the body, the person, and everything else. More often then not, the whole lot keeps functioning as it always did. Things like the original programming to speak a certain language, to enjoy certain music, and a taste for certain foods, usually remain intact.

Seeing through the ego/body/identity illusion, does not cancel death and taxes for the body/mind. There might be a relaxation, less investment in the story, but this does not imply that one now stops eating, drinking and sleeping. The mind/thinking process will still function in the pairs of opposites, and the ego, seen for what it is, might just keep its 'job' but is no longer considered as what you exclusively are.

This recognition is not 'done' by a person, as it is THAT what recognizes the person. It is pure (re)cognition, without someone doing the (re)cognizing, just as there is no 'it' that does the raining when 'it' rains.

In the body, the four elements combine: earth – in the form of food – water, air, and the fire of the metabolic process. Obviously, when the 'food element' is no longer supplied the body soon perishes, but THAT which lives AS the body never perishes. This Intelligent Essence – without which the body is just a corpse, is what you truly are. IT beats the heart, renews the cells, and digests the food, without the help of an I/ego.

Seeing through the magician's trick does not change the nature of the coin. Seeing through the illusion of the body/mind identity does not change the natural functioning of the body/mind. It will stay around for a while and, when it reaches its end, the four elements return to the four elements. The Life-Essence, the Animating Energy, is not affected by this; much as electricity is not affected when a light bulb burns out.

With Awakening comes the realization that you are not just the light bulb, or the light in the lamp, but the electricity that manifests as this light. While it is clear that there never was a person confined to the lamp/body, it usually does not translate in an urge to interfere with the natural functioning of the body/mind.

∾ ∾ ∾

When I'm hungry, I eat, when I'm tired I sleep.
Fools laugh at me. But the wise understand.

~ Rinzai Roku ~

85. How can Awareness be present during deep sleep?

Question: In the book 'Awakening to the Dream' it is said, more than once, that Pure Awareness is ever-present. But how can Awareness be present during deep sleep when there is no object to be aware of?

Answer: One way to answer this is by comparing Awareness and the objects of Awareness to hearing and sound. Ultimately, Awareness and its objects, hearing and sound, are indivisible, but for the sake of communication they appear here as two sides of the 'coin of Oneness.'

Provided that you're not suffering from deafness, the faculty of hearing is present even when there is no sound to be heard. We could as easily say that, at such times, silence is 'heard.' As soon as a sound arises the hearing becomes manifest. In the same way that the ability to hear is there, even during absolute silence, Awareness is present even when there is nothing to be aware of.

When this is clear, deep sleep is no longer seen as the absence of Awareness, but recognized as object-free Pure Awareness.

∽ ∽ ∽

This heart is known by the word 'I' in our daily experience.

Even when the ego is forgotten in deep sleep, it continues as its foundational being.

From : 'Upadeshasaram: The Essence of Instruction of BhagavanSriRamana Maharshi.' Available from: http://www.vedanet.com/Upadesha.htm

86. Nothing happened

Question: I wonder why some writers/speakers on non-duality insist that 'nothing happened' when asked about their apparent leap into clarity or awakening.

I understand that from the perspective of Oneness, Wholeness, Noumenon etc, nothing happened or ever has or will.

However, those putting such a question are inquiring from the perspective of phenomena. And from that perspective something did indeed appear to happen. An apperception occurred that reorganized the organism's perception of life. Perhaps it was a direct seeing into the impossibility of a self that could awaken. Perhaps it was the understanding that it is a contradiction in terms to speak of being alive and at the same time unawake.

It seems to me that there is always a neuronal leap involved, after which it's impossible to perceive the world or oneself in the 'old way' again. It's like the leap that occurs when a brain understands a wholly new body of knowledge and the way it jigsaws together.

I realize the dangers inherent in speaking of a 'happening' - how a legion of assumptions can constellate around it, turning it into an attainment by an entity in time and space and so on. But is denial of apperception as an apparent event a truthful pointer?

Answer: There are a few problems with describing the 'awakening event', including the fact − as you pointed out − from the absolute perspective nothing happened.

What you call 'the apparent event' is an experience, which comes in many guises. It may be a big bang or a subtle shift, or anything in between.

Pointing to an event is, however, very misleading, as IT is not about an event but about recognizing the Aware Space in which all events and phenomena arise and subside.

To talk about the 'awakening event' has often undesirable side-effects. People start to compare it to their own experiences and then say 'Oh, that did not happen to me, so I have to wait/try/hope/seek more in order to have such an experience.' It sets up comparison and longing, envy, hope and miserable feelings of 'still not there.' It focuses on the side-effects instead of on the essence.

Awakening shows that there is not now, nor was there ever, someone to become awakened. There are, however, people who had wonderful experiences and think that that is awakening/enlightenment. They can talk and write about it in a beautiful way, and perhaps they'll tell you that you can have it too, if only you do the same things they did. Awakening makes it clear that we are the inexperience-able experiencing itself and that each and every experience (including a mystical peak experience) is fleeting and temporal.

I was at a meeting where Tony Parsons mentioned how IT struck when he was walking in a park in England. All of a sudden everybody became interested in the experience and someone even wanted to know where that park was (half jokingly) so that he could go there and perhaps have a similar experience.

In the right context 'the experience' can be discussed, but the paradox is, that it is clear that it is not about the experience at all, that there is no one to have it and that placing it somewhere in time is actually incorrect. It is seen that it is pure and total Presence, and that Presence did not come about at a certain moment in time, but simply IS.

Question 2: Aren't certitudes about the wondrous, incomprehensible workings of Consciousness somehow an indication of inability to move beyond conceptualization?

Answer: The verbal expression of certitudes is always conceptual and concepts cannot go beyond concepts. Nevertheless, certainty itself is not a concept. For example: the knowing that you are is not a concept, but the expression of that knowing through – and as – the mind via the words 'I AM' is conceptual. Before the words 'I AM' were learned, the Beingness had to be there. This Beingness is a certainty.

Putting this into words, we end up with concepts. As long as this is known and we do not attempt to climb the signpost, there is no problem with this. In seeing concepts for what they are, it is recognized that the concept-generating mind can never move beyond the mind. On the other hand, THAT which you truly are does not need to move beyond conceptualization, because it already forever IS beyond and prior to conceptualization.

ᥟ᥏ ᥟ᥏ ᥟ᥏

It is there, it is immediate, it is there with you right now, without any conceptualization on it. Just pure ordinary, commonplace everyday awareness.

'Sailor' Bob Adamson on his website at: http://members.iinet.net.
au/~adamson7/index.html

87. One Source

Question: Since there is only the One Source appearing as everything, then are the Bible, the Creation Story and Jesus just myths, legends, or fairy stories or are they real in the sense that it is the One Source appearing as these too?

Answer: The past, in which creation appeared, in which the Bible was written, and in which Jesus walked the earth, is a story appearing presently. All there is is Source appearing right now. This implies that, in a sense, history is nothing but a collection of myths, legends and fairy stories, and yet, it is all the expression of Source. None of it has a separate existence, just as dreams do not exist apart from the dreamer.

All that appears is a single, magical, multi-dimensional, super hologram, including minds via which it projects endless labels on itself, such as; raindrops, cows, evolution theories, creationism, flowers, clouds, wars, angels, mountains, airplanes, galaxies, fireflies, and apple pies, to name but a few.

As such the Bible, Jesus and the creation story are as real or unreal as any other 'part' of this manifestation, and like everything else they can be seen as pointers to the primary 'screen' of Awareness on which it all appears.

Is it not the Bible in which it is written that God is omnipresent? If this is understood to be true, then who or what could ever be apart from God or Source?

This reminds me of a small anecdote about an Indian sage:

One day a sage was sitting in a temple and his foot was pointing to the statue of Shiva. Pointing one's foot to the temple deity is considered bad manners in India. A priest, who noticed the offending foot, furiously told the sage to not point it at Shiva. The sage gently replied: 'Dear, I'll gladly point my foot away from Shiva, if you can show me where he is not.'

Shiva, God, Source, the One, is prior to all conceptual divisions such as real and unreal. Whether it is realized or not, all that is ever seen or known is only the One seeing and knowing.

∾ ∾ ∾

I am the Light
Which illumines all men.
I am the All.
The All came forth from me
And the All ended up in me.
Split some wood, I am there.
Lift a stone, you will find me there.

From: 'The Gospel of Thomas' as translated by Jean-Yves Leloup

88. Is there any spontaneity to life?

Question: I read the newsletter when it comes and very much enjoy it. It and other books similar to yours have relaxed my seeking. I understand that there is no 'I' to even write this e-mail and no 'you' to respond to it. My question is, is there any spontaneity and/or chance to life, or is the entire process written in stone?

Answer: 'That Which Is' can be seen as the unavoidable outcome of previous causes. When that perspective is believed we can say it is all written in stone. On the other hand 'That What Is' can be seen as Uncaused Presence; including and transcending the idea of cause and effect. As such we can say that it is all unadulterated spontaneity, arising out of no-thing-ness, like bubbles in a glass of Champagne.

Stories of cause and effect, or theories of a spontaneous unfolding versus determinism, are itself part of 'That Which Is'. They are simply temporal points of view, which could be endlessly argued for or against.

Such stories are the mind's attempt to get a handle on existence and file it away, once and for all, under labels like 'spontaneously happening' or 'written in stone.'

Outside any perspective or labeling is the Untouched Mystery of Being. IT is expressing as all possible qualifications, and yet is forever free of them. Undisturbed by ideas of 'either/or' is this 'Isness that Is' and You Are That.

∾ ∾ ∾

'Out beyond ideas of right doing and wrong doing there is a field. I will meet you there.'

~ Rumi ~

89. Boldly go where no 'I' has gone before

Question: I have read your book which was a very interesting read. I just have a question about it if that's ok.

Would you say that it does not matter what a person does in life as regards trying to improve himself? Will success or failure happen regardless of what I try to do myself?

I don't know whether to try hard to improve my finances, emotions and life situation or not. For example, I keep thinking if I don't try to make things better for myself my life will not improve. I don't want to regret not having acted on the need to make an effort to improve things.

I realize that I do not really exist, but in terms of the dream, I would like my life to improve in many ways. I guess I would feel different if the ego dropped away for the apparent me.

I find it is difficult also to decide what or how I could improve things. Does it not matter, as what is, is? Whatever I apparently decide will be or not be? I just feel like I will not have a good enjoyable life unless I put effort in to improve it in some way. I don't want to miss out on what I could have done by not taking action, you see.

In a way it would be a lot easier if pre-destination did exist. That way I would know that I could not do anything to change things and therefore there would be no regret at all.

I would really appreciate it if you could share any

comments on the above points.

Answer: The text of 'Awakening to the Dream' does not state that improvement of personal circumstances is impossible, but that there is no separate 'you' to do it. When improvements happen they happen, and if this seems to include personal action and input then that is what happens. Here – and in 'Awakening to the Dream' – it is said that there is no 'you' having a life, but only life appearing as everything including the pattern identified as 'you.'

When we compare life to a river, then such a 'you pattern' is much like one of the ripples or bubbles which appear on the stream's surface. They are but temporal appearances on the river and do not have an independent existence. The invitation extended here is to recognize that there is only the river of life, and that your true identity is nothing less than the whole river.

When there is an urge to improve one's financial status or to learn a new language, or whatever, then that is the way life appears to itself and there is no 'you' in charge of this. Every thought, every action, every heartbeat, every breath is from and by the One only. The person as the doer and the possessor of 'my' life is again but a pattern in the stream you are.

See how often 'I' and 'myself' feature in your email. This 'I' seems to want, hope, fear, and decide. It seems to be the centre and the root of all doubt. When this is acknowledged, it can be investigated thoroughly. Don't accept anyone's words, and don't just say 'I realize I don't really exist' but really find out if this is so.

The word salt is not salty, but points to an actuality which cannot be captured in words. The word 'I' is not what you are but points to – and is an expression of – THAT which you are. Find out if this is so.

If or when it's clear where this 'I' concept points to, then there is no conceptual 'I' to understand this. In the end, when the conceptual 'I' doing the understanding cannot be found, understanding miraculously remains as an expression of 'your' True Nature.

See through the idea of being this body, this character, this collection of ideas and habits; boldly go where no 'I' has gone before, and re-cognize the Freedom-You-Are.

∽ ∽ ∽

The scriptures even proclaim aloud:'There is in truth no creation and no destruction; no one is bound, no one is seeking Liberation, no one is on the way to Deliverance. There are none liberated. This is the absolute truth.'

My dear disciple, this, the sum and substance of all the Upanishads, the secret of secrets, is my instruction to you.

From: 'Teachings of the Hindu Mystics' by Shankaracharya.
edited by Andrew Harvey, ISBN 1-57602-449-6

90. What about channelling?

Question: Since reading the books by Tony Parsons my search seems to be over.

The last step before that was reading channelled messages about the new energy and the light body and so forth, and attending a 'school of consciousness of the new time' via scripts and cds of channeled messages of ascended masters, angels and, and, and... The 'mind' seems to be very tricky in holding me in the play. And there is nothing wrong with that, because it's just Oneness appearing in so many different shapes.

Nevertheless I'd like to ask you whether you could say something about this whole theme out of clarity.

Answer: There is only IT appearing as everything; only Oneness appearing AS diversity. Channelling ascended masters, considering light bodies, tasting apple sauce, and seeing flying saucers, are all appearances with no independent existence. They are in fact nothing but temporal patterns in the current of life.

Look at the screen, rather than at the flickering images that appear on it. What is pointed to here is the mirror of Awareness, rather than the reflections in it. The images in the mirror cannot be brushed away, nor can they be taken hold of. They are both there and not there, and their apparent presence or absence does not affect the mirror in any way.

It is fine to be fascinated by the content of the mirror, and it is fine to be fascinated by the stories of ascending masters and light beings. They are as real or unreal as any other appearance, including the seeming person fascinated by such ideas.

༄ ༄ ༄

As thou reviewest the world with thy perfect intelligence and compassion, it must seem to thee like a dream of which it cannot be said: it is permanent or it is destructible, for being and non-being do not apply to it.

~ Lankavatara Sutra ~

91. How to go forward?

Question: Hi, I hope you can clarify some thoughts of mine.

Since I (as an individual) do not really exist, how do I go about living in an environment of people who actually don't exist? For what purpose would it serve other than Pure Awareness experiencing its earthly dream of 'being' different characters?

If everything around this 'me' are the experiences of Pure Awareness, then anything 'I' do really doesn't matter, right? If this is so, how do 'I' as a conscious being, existing in a dream, go about living this dream life with any joy?

I believe what you have said in your book is true. I just don't know how to go forward now that I realize I don't exist... do I just suck it up, the good along with the bad, and accept that my participation is inconsequential?

Answer: Please do not simply believe what I have said in the book, but verify it. Also remember that the words are no more than pointers to something beyond the reach of words; just like the lake is beyond the signpost that points to it. Obviously, when you want to go for a swim, merely believing, instead of following the direction indicated by the signpost, will not result in a refreshing dip in the water.

If it is actually clear that there is no individual, then who is there to believe what was written? Who needs to go forward, and who needs to participate?

The 'message' in these words may same bleak from the

'I' perspective. It seems to suggest meaninglessness and helplessness, but this is not to where the signpost points.

When it is seen that all activity is of the One, then it is also seen that this has always been the case. We may say things like 'I think.' or 'I breathe', but on investigation it is clear that every thought, every breath, every act, has never been done by a separate you and yet, here you are. Even the idea of a separate 'you' is 'done' by the One; just as a wave is 'done' by the ocean.

To the mind this may seem like losing the initiative, but in reality it never was the possessor of the initiative. You are not simply a limited character, but THAT to – and in which – the idea of such a character appears.

Seeing this is again not done by a 'you' but it is the One Seeing. To the 'person' this adds up to helplessness, and it is the end of who or what we think we are. However, since we are not what we think we are, it is only the end of an illusion. The separate person was never real, so it is the end of a non-existing entity. It all adds up to zero.

When there is a falling back into the Source, it turns out to be liberation rather then obliteration; liberation from doership and authority, from blame and fame. Instantly life is known to be effortlessly living AS you, and no longer as being lived BY you.

Presently, the thoughts appear and disappear, there is breathing in and out, the heart beats and the metabolism does its job. All this is directly seen without a 'someone' making an effort. There is no 'you' who is doing any of this and there never was, yet everything is going on by and of itself.

Participating, as you call it, may happen or not, but only as a play in Consciousness, as there is no real separation that allows for an independent participator or doer. Perhaps there will be a walk in the woods, a cup of tea, reading the newspaper, a dark mood, a smile, or doing the shopping; again, all happening AS you, rather than by or to you.

In and through all this spontaneous activity there might be the same surprised wonder as expressed by the Zen monk who, on finding out that there is no personal doer, wrote:

> *'Miraculous power and marvelous activity! Drawing water and hewing wood.'*

∾ ∾ ∾

This is the open secret, which all can discover for themselves. We live our lives, as it were'inside out,' projecting the existence of an 'I' as separate from an external world which we try to manipulate to gain satisfaction. But as long as one remains in the dualistic state, one's experience has always underlying it a sense of loss, of fear, of anxiety, and dissatisfaction. When, on the other hand, one goes beyond the dualistic level, anything is possible.

Chogyal Namkhai Norbu in 'The Crystal and the Way of Light'
ISBN: 1559391359

92. Journey's end

Question: Like many my 'journey' has covered numerous philosophies, teachers and countries, but for the moment it has ground to a halt.

The whole 'spiritual' scene has become so commercialized; how is one able to discern the truth from the bullshit, when we know we can't trust our minds?

Answer: If this is known then trust That which knows that the mind cannot be trusted; at least not when it comes to the clarity you seek. However, the mind can be instrumental in bringing you to the edge. It can understand that it could never think itself beyond thought. It can see that its functioning depends on – and is limited to – the pairs of opposites. It can see that it deals with labels and that the thought 'sugar' has no real taste.

Question: There are many people selling their 'methods' of reaching peace/Presence/truth for large sums of money – a Swami in India promises enlightenment for $5,000.

Answer: It is well known that there are such excesses. The mind may not be the right tool to grasp Oneness, but it's great for spotting dubious situations like this. Together with your intuition it has alerted you that such an offer is total bullshit.

This reminds me: a while back someone asked me what I thought about charging money for sharing this nondual perspective. Here is what I wrote:

'There is a saying that goes "For the time of your life, live the life of your time." In the illusory past, there were mountain hermits, wandering sages and secluded forests. There were sages living in caves and villagers bringing them food and offerings, but all that is rapidly fading away. Today there is air travel, printing presses, the internet, tax papers, and shopping malls.'

I never saw anything wrong with compensating those who are available to write about this, to answer questions, or to publicly meet and speak. Non-dual or not, costs are accrued, time is dedicated, and there are bills to be paid.

Such people may or may not be helpful to 'your' awakening, but in the end the certainty that you are THIS comes from the Living Centre, not from any person 'out there.' With this realization comes the seeing that there never was a 'you' on the path, nor are there 'others' who can give you what you already are. The one seeking, and the one pointing, is the same One, appearing as both apparent characters. Your True Nature is the 'puppeteer' moving both – and all – players.

Question: Others are a little more subtle but teach that enlightenment is a state in which you are always happy/in bliss (i.e. a state other than what we spend most of our time in!). We could be forgiven for thinking enlightenment is a state which can be gained or lost.

Answer: Yes, the suggestion of a 'bigger and better later on' is frequently made, but sometimes it is also understood as such; even when this is not what's being pointed out. For example, hearing that one is not the doer can result in attempts to 'do' non-doership. On hearing that one IS the sought after peace and freedom right now, some may call off the search, while others renew their efforts to reach this peace and freedom later on.

Question: Doing anything to reach a different 'state' is like trying to move out of the space we are in (and about as futile). If 'THAT' is all there is, how could it not encompass ALL states?

Answer: We say 'I breathe, I think, I feel', but it all happens by itself. The 'I' supposedly doing the thinking, is itself a part of the thought 'I think.' When, on investigation, the doer is not found, it becomes clear that there is no one doing anything; yet, everything gets done. Other states are 'reached' all the time, but even though IT has been called the Natural State or the Stateless State, IT is not really a state for a separate someone to be in; IT is the 'Eternal-Empty-Screen' on which all temporal states arise and subside. As such IT does indeed encompass *all* states.

Your space metaphor is a great pointer to this Stateless State, otherwise 'known' as the Knowing-Centre-That-Cannot-Be-Known. In Oneness, who could stand apart from IT as a knower?

You have no independent existence from THIS, in the same way that the hero in a theatre play does not have existence apart from the actor portraying him. There is nothing the hero can or has to do to become one with the actor; all that has to be seen is that he IS the actor, and the actor is HE. All the hero's deeds, thoughts and actions are then known not to be his at all, as they belong to the actor only.

In the same way, there is nothing you can or have to do to become one with the One Substance. IT appears to and of itself as this temporal manifestation, assuming all possible shapes and forms. IT appears as stars, saints, sinners, sages, seekers and AS you. When there is the recognition of this One-Essence, shapes and forms take a backseat to the acknowledgment of this Essence as THAT which you always, already, and truly are.

∞ ∞ ∞

These our actors,
As I foretold you, were all spirits and
Are melted into air, into thin air:
And, like the baseless fabric of this vision,
The cloud-capp'd towers, the gorgeous palaces,
The solemn temples, the great globe itself,
Yea, all which it inherit, shall dissolve
And, like this insubstantial pageant faded,
Leave not a rack behind. We are such stuff
As dreams are made of, and our little life
Is rounded with a sleep.

William Shakespeare, 'The Tempest', Act IV, Scene 1

Afterword

As you hold this book in your hands, the beginning and end of it are present right now. In between the covers, words repeatedly point to something beyond words. This 'something' is actually not a thing and therefore we may point to it as 'no-thing'.

Don't let these words fool you. Words pointing beyond words may sound mysterious, but just think about it for a second: With the possible exception of the word 'word', do not all words point to something beyond words? The word 'sweetness' is not sweet but, once tasted, we know what the word 'sweetness' indicates.

The words in this book repeatedly point to the essence which knows the reading as it takes place. Rather than an encouragement to follow a lengthy path, it is an invitation to step off the path. It does not point to 'your' awareness, but to Awareness itself in which the idea of 'you' appears. It does not point to 'your' beingness, but to the undeniable Beingness that appears as you.

Because this Beingness is all there is, because it is the very knowing that knows the reading of these words right now, they may 'hit the mark.' If they do, they are no longer needed and they become as superfluous as a list of directions for how to get to Paris, while viewing the city from the Eiffel Tower.

Dr. Richard B. Clarke graciously gave his permission to include his translation of the Hsin-hsin Ming in this book, and it seems a great way to end this writing.

All and nothing has been said.
Without beginning or end,
Everything is as it is;
Just This and nothing else.
All Clarity.
From Self to Self.

The Mind of Absolute Trust or the Hsin-hsin Ming

Translated by Richard B. Clarke

∾ ∾ ∾

The Great Way is not difficult for those not attached
to preferences.

When neither love nor hate arises, all is clear
and undisguised.

Separate by the smallest amount, however, and you
are as far from it as heaven is from earth.

If you wish to know the truth, then hold to no
opinions for or against anything.

To set up what you like against what you dislike
is the disease of the mind.

When the fundamental nature of things is not
recognized the mind's essential peace is disturbed to
no avail.

The Way is perfect as vast space is perfect,
where nothing is lacking and nothing is in excess.

Indeed, it is due to our grasping and rejecting
that we do not know the true nature of things.

Live neither in the entanglements of outer things,
nor in ideas or feelings of emptiness.

Be serene and at one with things and erroneous views
will disappear by themselves.

When you try to stop activity to achieve quietude,
your very effort fills you with activity.

As long as you remain attached to one extreme or
another you will never know Oneness.

Those who do not live in the Single Way cannot be
free in either activity or quietude, in assertion or denial.

Deny the reality of things and you miss their reality;
assert the emptiness of things and you miss their reality.

The more you talk and think about it the further you
wander from the truth.

So cease attachment to talking and thinking, and there is
nothing you will not be able to know.

To return to the root is to find the essence, but to pursue
appearances or 'enlightenment' is to miss the source.

To awaken even for a moment is to go beyond
appearance and emptiness.

Changes that seem to occur in the empty world we make
real only because of our ignorance.

Do not seek for the truth; only cease to cherish opinions.

Do not remain in a dualistic state; avoid such easy habits carefully.

If you attach even to a trace of this and that, of right and wrong, the Mind-essence will be lost in confusion.

Although all dualities arise from the One, do not be attached even to ideas of this One.

When the mind exists undisturbed in the Way, there is no objection to anything in the world; and when there is no objection to anything, things cease to be – in the old way.

When no discriminating attachment arises, the old mind ceases to exist.

Let go of things as separate existences and mind too vanishes.

Likewise when the thinking subject vanishes so too do the objects created by mind.

The arising of other gives rise to self; giving rise to self generates others.

Know these seeming two as facets of the One Fundamental Reality.

In this Emptiness, these two are really one – and each contains all phenomena.

If not comparing, nor attached to 'refined' and 'vulgar' –
you will not fall into judgment and opinion.

The Great Way is embracing and spacious – to live in it
is neither easy nor difficult.

Those who rely on limited views are fearful and
irresolute: the faster they hurry, the slower they go.

To have a narrow mind, and to be attached to getting
enlightenment is to lose one's centre and go astray.

When one is free from attachment, all things are as they
are, and there is neither coming nor going.

When in harmony with the nature of things, your own
fundamental nature, and you will walk freely and
undisturbed.

However, when mind is in bondage, the truth is
hidden, and everything is murky and unclear, and the
burdensome practice of judging brings annoyance and
weariness.

What benefit can be derived from attachment to
distinctions and separations?

If you wish to move in the One Way, do not dislike the
worlds of senses and ideas.

Indeed, to embrace them fullyis identical with true
Enlightenment.

The wise person attaches to no goals but the foolish person fetters himself or herself.

There is one Dharma, without differentiation. Distinctions arise from the clinging needs of the ignorant.

To seek Mind with the discriminating mind is the greatest of mistakes.

Rest and unrest derive from illusion; with enlightenment, attachment to liking and disliking ceases.

All dualities come from ignorant inference.

They are like dreams, phantoms, hallucinations – it is foolish to try to grasp them.

Gain and loss, right and wrong; finally abandon all such thoughts at once.

If the eye never sleeps, all dreams will naturally cease.

If the mind makes no discriminations, the ten thousand things are as they are, of single essence.

To realize the mystery of this One-essence is to be released from all entanglements.

When all things are seen without differentiation, the One Self-essence is everywhere revealed.

No comparisons or analogies are possible in this

causeless, relationless state of just this One.

When movement stops, there is no movement– and when no movement, there is no stopping.

When such dualities cease to exist Oneness itself cannot exist.

To this ultimate state no law or description applies.

For the Realized mind at one with the Way all self-centered striving ceases.

Doubts and irresolutions vanish and the Truth is confirmed in you.

With a single stroke you are freed from bondage; nothing clings to you and you hold to nothing.

All is empty, clear, self-illuminating, with no need to exert the mind.

Here, thinking, feeling, understanding, and imagination are of no value.

In this world 'as it really is' there is neither self nor other-than-self.

To know this Reality directly is possible only through practicing non-duality.

When you live this non-separation, all things manifest the One, and nothing is excluded.

Whoever comes to enlightenment, no matter when or where, realizes personally this fundamental Source.

This Dharma-truth has nothing to do with big or small, with time and space. Here a single thought is as ten thousand years.

Not here, not there – but everywhere always right before your eyes. Infinitely large and infinitely small: no difference, for definitions are irrelevant and no boundaries can be discerned.

So likewise with 'existence' and 'non-existence.'

Don't waste your time in arguments and discussion attempting to grasp the ungraspable.

Each thing reveals the One, the One manifests as all things.

To live in this Realization is not to worry about perfection nor non-perfection.

To put your trust in the Heart-Mind is to live without separation, and in this non-duality you are one with your Life-Source.

Words! Words! The Way is beyond language, for in it there is no yesterday, no tomorrow, no today.

By Seng-ts'an, Third Chan Patriarch, translated by Richard B. Clarke.
First published in 'Zen Bow,' magazine Vol. 1, No. 2, February 1968

About the Publisher

Non-Duality Press publishes book and audio resources on the theme of non-duality and *Advaita* with particular emphasis on works by contemporary speakers and authors.

For an up-to-date catalogue of books and CDs, with online ordering please visit: www. non-dualitybooks.com.

Other titles from Non-Duality Press include:

Awakening to the Dream: Leo Hartong

Shining in Plain View: John Wheeler

Awakening to the Natural State: John Wheeler

What's Wrong with Right Now? &

Presence-Awareness: 'Sailor' Bob Adamson

Already Awake: Nathan Gill

The POEMS *of*
ST. JOHN *of the* CROSS

These translations are dedicated

TO MARY

The POEMS of
ST. JOHN *of the* CROSS

The Spanish text
with a translation by

ROY CAMPBELL

Preface by
M. C. D'ARCY, S.J.

The Universal Library

GROSSET & DUNLAP
NEW YORK

The Spanish text of these poems is that of Padre Silverio de Santa Teresa, c.d. ('Obras de San Juan de la Cruz', Burgos, 1929-31), reprinted with his permission. It has previously appeared in England in 'San Juan de la Cruz: Poesías', Liverpool, Institute of Hispanic Studies, 1933, and in 'Poems of St John of the Cross', translated and edited by E. Allison Peers, London, Burns Oates, 1947. It is based on the Sanlúcar MS.

UNIVERSAL LIBRARY EDITION, 1967

BY ARRANGEMENT WITH
PANTHEON BOOKS, A DIVISION OF RANDOM HOUSE, INC.

PRINTED IN THE UNITED STATES OF AMERICA

Contents

PREFACE

MR ROY CAMPBELL lived long in Spain and in the years grew in his affection and admiration for the Spanish genius and its faith. It is not surprising, therefore, that as a poet he should have translated into English verse one of the great religious poets of Spain. St John of the Cross is an acknowledged master amongst Christian mystics, and a poet in his own right. Just as St Teresa of Avila has won a place in the literature of Spain by the freshness and humanity of her style, so among poets St John, her contemporary and devoted friend, is accepted as supreme in his *genre* by Spanish critics. In the great work of P. Silverio de Santa Teresa, translated and edited by Professor E. Allison Peers, the verdict of Menéndez y Pelayo is quoted. The passage is taken from an address on Mystical Poetry to the Spanish Academy: 'So sublime is this poetry that it scarcely seems to belong to this world at all; it is hardly capable of being assessed by literary criteria. More ardent in its passion than any profane poetry, its form is elegant and exquisite, as plastic and highly figured as any of the finest works of the Renaissance. The Spirit of God has passed through these poems every one, beautifying and sanctifying them on its way.'

For a long time interest in this country was so centred on St Teresa of Avila that St John stood in her shade. The nineteenth century was not seriously attracted to mysticism. Memories of its excesses still lingered: and St Teresa was read more because her character was irresistible than through a desire to follow her mystical way. As is well known, many leading Protestant divines refused to give mysticism a place within the Christian faith, and for a period Catholic spiritual writers advocated a vigorous practice of the virtues in preference to what savoured of illuminism or quietism. In the last fifty years this open or veiled hostility has changed in a marked degree to appreciation. The writings of Evelyn Underhill and Dean Inge stirred the interest of those outside the Catholic Church, while within the Church a host of writers, of whom I need mention only Baron Von Hügel, Abbot Butler, H. Bremond and P. Maréchal, gave a lead to a new and serious study of mystical writings. Among such writings those of St John of the Cross were bound to take a foremost place. They give what many consider the most complete and clear-cut description of the many stages in the mystical ascent.

St John of the Cross was far from any intention to describe his experiences. He was the humblest of men, tiny in body and most retiring of disposition. It was St Teresa who with her genius for reading souls saw through the exterior littleness into the greatness of his spirit, and she singled him out to do for men what she was heroically undertaking in the reform of the nuns of the Carmelite Order. His admiration for and love of St Teresa made him accept what was most repugnant to his nature, and the work he took on his shoulders brought him trials of every kind, many indignities, and even imprisonment by his outraged brethren. Without any preconceived idea of writing, he adopted the habit of jotting down maxims to help others, and at the request of those he thus helped he wrote out for their sake and guidance a treatise for souls entering on the mysterious paths of mystical prayer. Even when doing this he took care, as he thought, only to supplement what he felt St Teresa, with far greater sanctity and experience, was writing. It looks, however, as if the poems just escaped from him; they are stanzas of the spontaneous and semi-ecstatic love song he had always in his heart, once he had come to know God. Many of these poems seem to have been composed when he was imprisoned at Toledo. Others were written at Baeza, a place he loved because in the woods around and by the side of the river Guadalimar he could

[2]

pass happy hours in union with God. Later, while Prior at Granada, between 1582 and 1585, he wrote the last parts of his prose works as a commentary on the stanzas of the poems.

From this it would appear that poetry was more natural to him than prose: and this is confirmed by the testimony of a nun at the process of his canonization in 1618.* 'One day he asked this witness in what her prayer consisted, and she replied: "In considering the beauty of God and in rejoicing that He has such beauty." And the Saint was so pleased with this that for some days he said the most sublime things concerning the beauty of God, at which all marvelled. And thus, under the influence of this love, he composed five stanzas, beginning "Beloved let us sing, and in Thy beauty see ourselves portray'd." (*Rejoice, my love, with me*, p. 27.) And in all this he showed that there was in his breast a great love of God.' In this artless but vivid account we see how St John was taken out of himself by the simple words of another, and so moved that at the end the ecstasy spilled over into stanzas of love, the Bride crying to the Beloved:

> *Rejoice, my love, with me*
> *And in your beauty see us both reflected:*
> *By mountain-slope and lea*
> *Where purest rills run free,*
> *We'll pass into the forest undetected.*

In making his versions Mr Roy Campbell was able to go directly to the Spanish originals, and he was fortunate in that the original Spanish texts had then been edited with care and critical knowledge. For a long time a critical study of these texts was neglected, and readers of St John had to be content with an edition which had been first published in 1703. The well-known English translation by David Lewis, published in 1889, had to be based on this unschol-

*Quoted in *The Complete Works of St John of The Cross*, edited by E. Allison Peers, London, Burns Oates, 1934-5.

arly text. Fortunately a band of Carmelites in Spain set to work to give us an accurate and authentic text, and they were helped by Fr Benedict Zimmerman and Professor Allison Peers in England. To the latter we owe many important studies on the great Spanish Mystics and also a translation of the truly scientific and recent text in Spanish by P. Silverio de Santa Teresa. Allison Peers in this translation has given us a rendering of the poems in what he himself describes as a 'long and metrically unfettered verse-line'. The great merit of this form of translation is that it serves to let the true likeness of St John appear and avoids the disguise imposed by prose. It also leaves the way open for a poet to try to turn into equivalent English verse what St John has done in Spanish, and moreover to capture the very spirit of the original as Crashaw tried to do with St Teresa.

To do this is a most difficult undertaking. Mystical experience is caviare to the general: it is attained only by the denial of all that we commonly call experience. A new world is discovered which is so different from our familiar one that all our words drawn from our ordinary and familiar experience fail to describe it. They would seem bound in fact to give a wrong impression, as they make us think of what we know instead of this new unknown. In a sense, undoubtedly, mystical experience is ineffable: it would not be that experience if the words used to tell of it were common to it and what we already know. Even within the multiple experience which we all share it is extremely hard to communicate what we may have felt. A man may want to tell us what he felt when he was listening to some music or after meeting someone he loves, or when he met death face to face for the first time; or he may wish to tell us the effect on him of a drug or a spasm of pain or the joy of an unexpected success. The experience is to him unique and all the words he uses could be applicable to something else. It would be easy to argue that private experiences are quite incommunicable; and yet the mysterious fact is that there is a human art of communication which somehow or other overcomes the seemingly insuperable obstacle. The good artist knows that sound and taste, for instance, will help to tell the truth about sight, that we can feel colour and transpose sight into sound. Moreover, by assonances and associations and by change of rhythm and by heightening the power of words and enlisting our sympathy, he can enable us to relive his own individual experience; and this is precisely what the poet or the great artist does. This is his magic, his gift from God. And this is why neither St John of the Cross nor a translator, like Roy Campbell, refrains from putting into the language of verse what is in itself far more difficult to communicate than the most personal of ordinary human experiences.

To appreciate intelligently the songs of a mystic like St John of the Cross it is essential to grasp the nature of true mysticism. Otherwise such words as

> *Reveal your presence clearly*
> *And kill me with the beauty you discover,*
> *For pains acquired so dearly*
> *From Love, cannot recover*
> *Save only through the presence of the lover.*

will in all likelihood be thought to be the description of an intense and very human emotion of the love we know. The truth is that this mystical love cannot even begin until the emotions we are thinking of have been hushed and put to sleep. In our everyday life we are both active and passive, and this is seen very well in our relations with others. They influence our thoughts and behaviour when we are in their presence. A frightened man before an interview can dramatize to himself what he will do and what he will say; but in the interview itself he feels the impact of the other and despite himself may be overpowered by the other's character. Again, our love for the long dead must be very strong for their influence to remain with us and touch us as if they were still alive and present. Now normally we cannot feel any contact with disembodied spirit, and if there be any truth in the supposed communications with the dead, it should be noticed that the contact is on the level of our ordinary sight and by sensible words. In religion, as God is supreme Spirit, our knowledge of Him is indirect, that is to say, by faith or true report. But St John, following the line of the great mystics, in his commentaries on his poems explains how with the grace of God those who are drawn to contemplation may experience the presence of God in a way comparable to that which we enjoy when our friends meet us. The way, however, is exceedingly arduous, so arduous, in fact, as to terrify all except the bravest of lovers. It comes to this, that we must surrender all that is dearest to us in the enjoyment of the senses and go through a dark night in which we live without their help and comfort. Then when this is accomplished we have to sacrifice the prerogative of our own way of thinking and willing and undergo another still darker night in which we have deprived ourselves of all the supports which are familiar to us and make us self-sufficient. This is a kind of death, the making nothing of all that we are to ourselves; but the genuine mystic tells us that when all has been strained away our emptiness will be filled with a new presence; our uncovered soul will receive the contact of divine love, and a new circuit of love will begin, when the soul is passive to an indescribable love which is given to it.

This experience is as remote as can be from the hot life of the senses or even the exalted sharing of human love. Nevertheless just because God is love and man was made in the image of God, the symbolism of human love can be turned to use and made to describe what are the effects of mystical union. How this can be done only a Saint like St John of the Cross can tell us, and he does so by so using language that we know all the time how the images of lover

and beloved, bridegroom and bride, the *clichés* of love we
might almost say, are no more exact than pointer readings;
they are copper coins acting as currency for silver. The
touch of God is entirely spiritual, and the soul is touched
at its source below the level of its activities of thought and
will. It is true that the love aroused by this contact may
overflow into the emotions and the body and so charge
any words used with a supernatural sense, but all the same
great artistry and holiness must combine to etherialize the
passionate words of sense and make us feel that they have
been dipped in some divine spring. There are those who
will refuse to believe that this mystical verse is anything
more than concealed human passion, and such critics
persuade themselves that saints, like St John of the Cross,
are victims of some pathological disorder. There is not
the slightest evidence for this, so far as I know, in the life
of St John, and we have his quiet and strong commentaries on his poems to prove to us what he had in mind
when he wrote the poems. To those who have ears to
hear, the accents of a genuine experience are unmistakable,
and the unprejudiced reader must, I think, become
conscious of an unearthly glow in the verse, a strange
quality which invades the images and persuades him that
there must be a love which is a secret between God and the
soul.

In writing this I am assuming that this quality pervades
also the translation which Mr Roy Campbell made of the
original Spanish. The reader will be made to realize what
the original Spanish is like, how truly a poet St John of the
Cross is, and he will, I hope, feel the freshness and the
intensity of the mystic and see how the verse leaves the
ground and soars to the heights without passing beyond
our sight. The ecstatic poems have, too, a movement and
metre which belong very closely to the mood, and these
have been caught in the translation. The best known of all
is the *En Una Noche Oscura*, and we can feel the hush of

darkness and the flight of the soul up the secret stair. The Stanzas of the *Spiritual Canticle* are almost equally well known and should be still more appreciated now that the images used stand out in their amazing clarity—that, for instance, of the bridegroom:

> *Turn, Ringdove, and alight,*
> *The wounded stag above*
> *The slope is now in sight*
> *Fanned by the wind and freshness of your flight.*

In some more measured poems St John combines the theme of love with a statement of some of the Christian mysteries. These make a demand on any translator because extreme accuracy of theological language has to be worked in with the exigencies of the verse. Here we are reminded of the skill of St Thomas Aquinas in composing the *Lauda Sion* and the *Sacris Solemnis*. Lastly there are those poems with refrains, such as, ' And die because I do not die ', and ' Transcending knowledge with my Thought '. Mr Campbell has been most happy, perhaps, in these, because they seem to float so easily into a pattern which some of the greatest English poets have used. Perfect translation hides the sense of translation, and who would guess that such a stanza as the following is not an original?

> *This life I live in vital strength*
> *Is loss of life unless I win You:*
> *And thus to die I shall continue*
> *Until I live in You at length.*
> *Listen (my God!) my life is in You.*
> *This life I do not want, for I*
> *Am dying that I do not die.*

By rising to this level and maintaining it Mr Roy Campbell carries us with him to Spain and into the presence of a Saint singing of the love of God. He proves, also, as other English poets have proved, that translation can be a stimulus and an original pleasure to a genuine poet.

M. C. D'ARCY, S.J.

[8]

POESÍAS—POEMS

I

Canciones del alma que se goza de haber llega-
do al alto estado de la perfección, que es la
unión con Dios, por el camino de la negación
espiritual

En una noche oscura,
Con ansias en amores inflamada,
¡Oh dichosa ventura!
Salí sin ser notada,
Estando ya mi casa sosegada.

A escuras, y segura,
Por la secreta escala disfrazada,
¡Oh dichosa ventura!
A escuras, y en celada,
Estando ya mi casa sosegada.

En la noche dichosa,
En secreto, que nadie me veía,
Ni yo miraba cosa,
Sin otra luz y guía,
Sino la que en el corazón ardía.

Aquesta me guiaba
Más cierto que la luz del mediodía,
A donde me esperaba
Quien yo bien me sabía,
En parte donde nadie parecía.

¡Oh noche, que guiaste,
Oh noche amable más que el alborada:

I

*Songs of the soul in rapture at having
arrived at the height of perfection, which
is union with God by the road of spiritual
negation*

Upon a gloomy night,
With all my cares to loving ardours flushed,
(O venture of delight!)
With nobody in sight
I went abroad when all my house was hushed.

In safety, in disguise,
In darkness up the secret stair I crept,
(O happy enterprise)
Concealed from other eyes
When all my house at length in silence slept.

Upon that lucky night
In secrecy, inscrutable to sight,
I went without discerning
And with no other light
Except for that which in my heart was burning.

It lit and led me through
More certain than the light of noonday clear
To where One waited near
Whose presence well I knew,
There where no other presence might appear.

Oh night that was my guide!
Oh darkness dearer than the morning's pride,

[11]

Oh noche que juntaste
Amado con amada,
Amada en el Amado transformada!

En mi pecho florido,
Que entero para él sólo se guardaba,
Allí quedó dormido,
Y yo le regalaba,
Y el ventalle de cedros aire daba.

El aire de la almena,
Cuando yo sus cabellos esparcía,
Con su mano serena
En mi cuello hería,
Y todos mis sentidos suspendía.

Quedéme, y olvidéme,
El rostro recliné sobre el Amado,
Cesó todo, y dejéme,
Dejando mi cuidado
Entre las azucenas olvidado.

Oh night that joined the lover
To the beloved bride
Transfiguring them each into the other.

Within my flowering breast
Which only for himself entire I save
He sank into his rest
And all my gifts I gave
Lulled by the airs with which the cedars wave.

Over the ramparts fanned
While the fresh wind was fluttering his tresses,
With his serenest hand
My neck he wounded, and
Suspended every sense with its caresses.

Lost to myself I stayed
My face upon my lover having laid
From all endeavour ceasing:
And all my cares releasing
Threw them amongst the lilies there to fade.

II

Canciones entre el alma y el Esposo

ESPOSA
¿A dónde te escondiste,
Amado, y me dejaste con gemido?
Como el ciervo huiste,
Habiéndome herido;
Salí tras ti clamando, y eras ido.

Pastores, los que fuerdes
Allá por las majadas al otero,
Si por ventura vierdes
Aquel que yo más quiero,
Decidle que adolezco, peno y muero.

Buscando mis amores,
Iré por esos montes y riberas,
Ni cogeré las flores,
Ni temeré las fieras,
Y pasaré los fuertes y fronteras.

PREGUNTA A LAS CRIATURAS
¡Oh bosques y espesuras,
Plantadas por la mano del Amado!
¡Oh prado de verduras,
De flores esmaltado,
Decid si por vosotros ha pasado!

RESPUESTA DE LAS CRIATURAS
Mil gracias derramando,
Pasó por estos sotos con presura,
Y yéndolos mirando,
Con sola su figura
Vestidos los dejó de hermosura.

[14]

II

Songs between the soul and the bridegroom

BRIDE
Where can your hiding be,
Beloved, that you left me thus to moan
While like the stag you flee
Leaving the wound with me?
I followed calling loud, but you had flown.

O shepherds, you that, yonder,
Go through the sheepfolds of the slope on high,
If you, as there you wander,
Should chance my love to spy,
Then tell him that I suffer, grieve, and die.

To fetch my loves more near,
Amongst these mountains and ravines I'll stray,
Nor pluck flowers, nor for fear
Of prowling beasts delay,
But pass through forts and frontiers on my way.

QUESTION TO ALL CREATURES
O thickets, densely-trammelled,
Which my love's hand has sown along the height:
O field of green, enamelled
With blossoms, tell me right
If he has passed across you in his flight.

REPLY OF THE CREATURES
Diffusing showers of grace
In haste among these groves his path he took,
And only with his face,
Glancing around the place,
Has clothed them in his beauty with a look.

ESPOSA

¡Ay, quién podrá sanarme!
Acaba de entregarte ya de vero.
No quieras enviarme
De hoy más ya mensajero,
Que no saben decirme lo que quiero.

Y todos cuantos vagan,
De ti me van mil gracias refiriendo,
Y todos más me llagan,
Y déjame muriendo
Un no sé qué que quedan balbuciendo.

Mas, ¿cómo perseveras,
Oh vida, no viviendo donde vives,
Y haciendo porque mueras,
Las flechas que recibes,
De lo que del Amado en ti concibes?

¿Por qué, pues has llagado
A aqueste corazón, no le sanaste?
Y pues me le has robado,
¿Por qué así le dejaste,
Y no tomas el robo que robaste?

Apaga mis enojos,
Pues que ninguno basta a deshacellos,
Y véante mis ojos,
Pues eres lumbre dellos,
Y sólo para ti quiero tenellos.

Descubre tu presencia,
Y máteme tu vista y hermosura;
Mira que la dolencia
De amor, que no se cura
Sino con la presencia y la figura.

BRIDE

Oh who my grief can mend!
Come, make the last surrender that I yearn for,
And let there be an end
Of messengers you send
Who bring me other tidings than I burn for.

All those that haunt the spot
Recount your charm, and wound me worst of all
Babbling I know not what
Strange rapture, they recall,
Which leaves me stretched and dying where I fall.

How can you thus continue
To live, my life, where your own life is not?
With all the arrows in you
And, like a target, shot
By that which in your breast he has begot.

Why then did you so pierce
My heart, nor heal it with your touch sublime?
Why, like a robber fierce,
Desert me every time
And not enjoy the plunder of your crime?

Come, end my sufferings quite
Since no one else suffices for physician:
And let mine eyes have sight
Of you, who are their light,
Except for whom I scorn the gift of vision.

Reveal your presence clearly
And kill me with the beauty you discover,
For pains acquired so dearly
From Love, cannot recover
Save only through the presence of the lover.

¡Oh cristalina fuente,
Si en esos tus semblantes plateados,
Formases de repente
Los ojos deseados,
Que tengo en mis entrañas dibujados!

Apártalos, Amado,
Que voy de vuelo.

ESPOSO

Vuélvete, paloma,
Que el ciervo vulnerado
Por el otero asoma,
Al aire de tu vuelo, y fresco toma.

ESPOSA

Mi Amado, las montañas,
Los valles solitarios nemorosos,
Las ínsulas extrañas,
Los ríos sonorosos,
El silbo de los aires amorosos.

La noche sosegada
En par de los levantes de la aurora,
La música callada,
La soledad sonora,
La cena, que recrea y enamora.

Nuestro lecho florido,
De cuevas de leones enlazado,
En púrpura tendido,
De paz edificado,
De mil escudos de oro coronado.

O brook of crystal sheen,
Could you but cause, upon your silver fine,
Suddenly to be seen
The eyes for which I pine
Which in my inmost heart my thoughts design!

Withhold their gaze, my Love.
For I take wing.

THE BRIDEGROOM
        Turn, Ringdove, and alight,
The wounded stag above
The slope is now in sight
Fanned by the wind and freshness of your flight.

THE BRIDE
My Love's the mountain range,
The valleys each with solitary grove,
The islands far and strange,
The streams with sounds that change,
The whistling of the lovesick winds that rove.

Before the dawn comes round
Here is the night, dead-hushed with all its glamours,
The music without sound,
The solitude that clamours,
The supper that revives us and enamours.

Now flowers the marriage bed
With dens of lions fortified around it,
With tent of purple spread,
In peace securely founded,
And by a thousand shields of gold surmounted.

[19]

A zaga de tu huella
Las jóvenes discurren al camino
Al toque de centella,
Al adobado vino,
Emisiones de bálsamo Divino.

En la interior bodega
De mi amado bebí, y cuando salía
Por toda aquesta vega,
Ya cosa no sabía,
Y el ganado perdí, que antes seguía.

Allí me dió su pecho,
Allí me enseñó ciencia muy sabrosa,
Y yo le dí de hecho
A mí, sin dejar cosa;
Allí le prometí de ser su esposa.

Mi alma se ha empleado,
Y todo mi caudal en su servicio:
Ya no guardo ganado,
Ni ya tengo otro oficio;
Que ya sólo en amar es mi ejercicio.

Pues ya si en el ejido
De hoy más no fuere vista ni hallada,
Diréis que me he perdido,
Que andando enamorada,
Me hice perdidiza, y fuí ganada.

De flores y esmeraldas
En las frescas mañanas escogidas,
Haremos las guirnaldas,
En tu amor florecidas,
Y en un cabello mío entretejidas.

Tracking your sandal-mark
The maidens search the roadway for your sign,
Yearning to catch the spark
And taste the scented wine
Which emanates a balm that is divine.

Deep-cellared is the cavern
Of my love's heart, I drank of him alive:
Now, stumbling from the tavern,
No thoughts of mine survive,
And I have lost the flock I used to drive.

He gave his breast; seraphic
In savour was the science that he taught;
And there I made my traffic
Of all, withholding naught,
And promised to become the bride he sought.

My spirit I prepare
To serve him with her riches and her beauty.
No flocks are now my care,
No other toil I share,
And only now in loving is my duty.

So now if from this day
I am not found among the haunts of men,
Say that I went astray
Love-stricken from my way,
That I was lost, but have been found again.

Of flowers and emeralds sheen,
Collected when the dews of dawning shine,
A wreath of garlands green
(That flower for you) we'll twine
Together with one golden hair of mine.

En solo aquel cabello,
Que en mi cuello volar consideraste,
Mirástele en mi cuello,
Y en él preso quedaste,
Y en uno de mis ojos te llagaste.

Cuando tú me mirabas,
Tu gracia en mí tus ojos imprimían:
Por eso me adamabas,
Y en eso merecían
Los míos adorar lo que en ti vían.

No quieras despreciarme,
Que si color moreno en mí hallaste,
Ya bien puedes mirarme,
Después que me miraste,
Que gracia y hermosura en mí dejaste.

Cogednos las raposas,
Que está ya florecida nuestra viña,
En tanto que de rosas
Hacemos una piña,
Y no parezca nadie en la montiña.

Detente, Cierzo muerto;
Ven, Austro, que recuerdas los amores,
Aspira por mi huerto,
Y corran sus olores,
Y pacerá el Amado entre las flores.

ESPOSO
Entrádose ha la Esposa
En el ameno huerto deseado,
Y a su sabor reposa,
El cuello reclinado
Sobre los dulces brazos del Amado.

[22]

One hair (upon my nape
You loved to watch it flutter, fall, and rise)
Preventing your escape,
Has snared you for a prize
And held you, to be wounded from my eyes.

When you at first surmised me
Your gaze was on my eyes imprinted so,
That it effeminized me,
And my eyes were not slow
To worship that which set your own aglow.

Scorn not my humble ways,
And if my hue is tawny do not loathe me.
On me you well may gaze
Since, after that, the rays
Of every grace and loveliness will clothe me.

Chase all the foxes hence
Because our vine already flowers apace:
And while with roses dense
Our posy we enlace,
Let no one on the hillside show his face.

Cease, then, you arctic gale,
And come, recalling love, wind of the South:
Within my garden-pale
The scent of flowers exhale
Which my Beloved browses with his mouth.

BRIDEGROOM
Now, as she long aspired,
Into the garden comes the bride, a guest:
And in its shade retired
Has leant her neck to rest
Against the gentle arm of the Desired.

[23]

Debajo del manzano,
Allí conmigo fuiste desposada,
Allí te dí la mano,
Y fuiste reparada,
Donde tu madre fuera violada.

A las aves ligeras,
Leones, ciervos, gamos saltadores,
Montes, valles, riberas,
Aguas, aires, ardores,
Y miedos de las noches veladores:

Por las amenas liras
Y canto de serenas os conjuro
Que cesen vuestras iras,
Y no toquéis al muro,
Porque la Esposa duerma más seguro.

ESPOSA

¡Oh ninfas de Judea,
En tanto que en las flores y rosales
El ámbar perfumea,
Morá en los arrabales,
Y no queráis tocar nuestros umbrales!

Escóndete, Carillo,
Y mira con tu haz a las montañas,
Y no quieras decillo:
Mas mira las compañas
De la que va por ínsulas extrañas.

ESPOSO

La blanca palomica
Al Arca con el ramo se ha tornado,
Y ya la tortolica
Al socio deseado
En las riberas verdes ha hallado.

[24]

Beneath the apple-tree,
You came to swear your troth and to be mated,
Gave there your hand to me,
And have been new-created
There where your mother first was violated.

You birds with airy wings,
Lions, and stags, and roebucks leaping light,
Hills, valleys, creeks, and springs,
Waves, winds, and ardours bright,
And things that rule the watches of the night:

By the sweet lyre and call
Of sirens, now I conjure you to cease
Your tumults one and all,
Nor echo on the wall
That she may sleep securely and at peace.

BRIDE

Oh daughters of Judea,
While yet our flowers and roses in their flesh hold
Ambrosia, come not here,
But keep the outskirts clear,
And do not dare to pass across our threshold.

Look to the mountain peak,
My darling, and stay hidden from the view,
And do not dare to speak
But watch her retinue
Who sails away to islands strange and new.

BRIDEGROOM

The dove so snowy-white,
Returning to the Ark, her frond bestows:
And seeking to unite
The mate of her delight
Has found him where the shady river flows.

[25]

En soledad vivía,
Y en soledad ha puesto ya su nido,
Y en soledad la guía
A solas su querido,
También en soledad de amor herido.

ESPOSA
Gocémonos, Amado,
Y vámonos a ver en tu hermosura
Al monte u al collado,
Do mana el agua pura;
Entremos más adentro en la espesura.

Y luego a las subidas
Cavernas de la piedra nos iremos,
Que están bien escondidas,
Y allí nos entraremos,
Y el mosto de granadas gustaremos.

Allí me mostrarías
Aquello que mi alma pretendía,
Y luego me darías
Allí tú, vida mía,
Aquello que me diste el otro día.

El aspirar del aire,
El canto de la dulce Filomena,
El soto y su donaire,
En la noche serena
Con llama que consume y no da pena.

Que nadie lo miraba,
Aminadab tampoco parecía,
Y el cerco sosegaba,
Y la caballería
A vista de las aguas descendía.

In solitude she bided,
And in the solitude her nest she made:
In solitude he guided
His loved-one through the shade
Whose solitude the wound of love has made.

BRIDE

Rejoice, my love, with me
And in your beauty see us both reflected:
By mountain-slope and lea,
Where purest rills run free,
We'll pass into the forest undetected:

Then climb to lofty places
Among the caves and boulders of the granite,
Where every track effaces,
And, entering, leave no traces,
And revel in the wine of the pomegranate.

Up there, to me you'll show
What my own soul has longed for all the way:
And there, my love, bestow
The secret which you know
And only spoke about the other day.

The breathing air so keen;
The song of Philomel: the waving charm
Of groves in beauty seen:
The evening so serene,
With fire that can consume yet do no harm.

With none our peace offending,
Aminadab has vanished with his slaughters:
And now the siege had ending,
The cavalcades descending
Were seen within the precinct of the waters.

III

Canciones del alma en la intima comunicación
de unión de amor de Dios. Del mismo auctor

¡Oh llama de amor viva,
Que tiernamente hieres
De mi alma en el más profundo centro!
Pues ya no eres esquiva,
Acaba ya si quieres,
Rompe la tela deste dulce encuentro.

¡Oh cauterio suave!
¡Oh regalada llaga!
¡Oh mano blanda! ¡Oh toque delicado,
Que a vida eterna sabe,
Y toda deuda paga!
Matando, muerte en vida la has trocado.

¡Oh lámparas de fuego,
En cuyos resplandores
Las profundas cavernas del sentido,
Que estaba obscuro y ciego,
Con extraños primores
Calor y luz dan junto a su querido!

¡Cuán manso y amoroso
Recuerdas en mi seno,
Donde secretamente solo moras:
Y en tu aspirar sabroso
De bien y gloria lleno
Cuán delicadamente me enamoras!

III

Song of the soul in intimate communication and union with the love of God

Oh flame of love so living,
How tenderly you force
To my soul's inmost core your fiery probe!
Since now you've no misgiving,
End it, pursue your course
And for our sweet encounter tear the robe!

Oh cautery most tender!
Oh gash that is my guerdon!
Oh gentle hand! Oh touch how softly thrilling!
Eternal life you render,
Raise of all debts the burden
And change my death to life, even while killing!

Oh lamps of fiery blaze
To whose refulgent fuel
The deepest caverns of my soul grow bright,
Late blind with gloom and haze,
But in this strange renewal
Giving to the belov'd both heat and light.

What peace, with love enwreathing,
You conjure to my breast
Which only you your dwelling place may call:
While with delicious breathings
In glory, grace, and rest,
So daintily in love you make me fall!

IV

Coplas del mismo hechas sobre un éxtasis de alta contemplación

Entréme donde no supe,
Y quedéme no sabiendo,
Toda sciencia trascendiendo.

Yo no supe dónde entraba,
Pero, cuando allí me ví,
Sin saber dónde me estaba,
Grandes cosas entendí;
No diré lo que sentí,
Que me quedé no sabiendo,
Toda sciencia trascendiendo.

De paz y de piedad
Era la sciencia perfecta,
En profunda soledad,
Entendida vía recta;
Era cosa tan secreta,
Que me quedé balbuciendo,
Toda sciencia trascendiendo.

Estaba tan embebido,
Tan absorto y ajenado,
Que se quedó mi sentido
De todo sentir privado;
Y el espíritu dotado
De un entender no entendiendo,
Toda sciencia trascendiendo.

El que allí llega de vero,
De sí mismo desfallesce;
Cuanto sabía primero

I V

Verses written after an ecstasy of high exaltation

I entered in, I know not where,
And I remained, though knowing naught,
Transcending knowledge with my thought.

Of when I entered I know naught,
But when I saw that I was there
(Though where it was I did not care)
Strange things I learned, with greatness fraught.
Yet what I heard I'll not declare.
But there I stayed, though knowing naught,
Transcending knowledge with my thought.

Of peace and piety interwound
This perfect science had been wrought,
Within the solitude profound
A straight and narrow path it taught,
Such secret wisdom there I found
That there I stammered, saying naught,
But topped all knowledge with my thought.

So borne aloft, so drunken-reeling,
So rapt was I, so swept away,
Within the scope of sense or feeling
My sense or feeling could not stay.
And in my soul I felt, revealing,
A sense that, though its sense was naught,
Transcended knowledge with my thought.

The man who truly there has come
Of his own self must shed the guise;
Of all he knew before the sum

Mucho bajo le paresce;
Y su sciencia tanto cresce,
Que se queda no sabiendo,
Toda sciencia trascendiendo.

Cuanto más alto se sube,
Tanto menos entendía
Qué es la tenebrosa nube
Que a la noche esclarecía;
Por eso quien la sabía
Queda siempre no sabiendo
Toda sciencia trascendiendo.

Este saber no sabiendo
Es de tan alto poder,
Que los sabios arguyendo
Jamás le pueden vencer;
Que no llega su saber
A no entender entendiendo,
Toda sciencia trascendiendo.

Y es de tan alta excelencia
Aqueste sumo saber,
Que no hay facultad ni sciencia
Que le puedan emprender;
Quien se supiere vencer
Con un no saber sabiendo,
Irá siempre trascendiendo.

Y si lo queréis oír,
Consiste esta suma sciencia
En un subido sentir
De la divinal Esencia;
Es obra de su clemencia
Hacer quedar no entendiendo
Toda sciencia trascendiendo.

Seems far beneath that wondrous prize:
And in this lore he grows so wise
That he remains, though knowing naught,
Transcending knowledge with his thought.

The farther that I climbed the height
The less I seemed to understand
The cloud so tenebrous and grand
That there illuminates the night.
For he who understands that sight
Remains for aye, though knowing naught,
Transcending knowledge with his thought.

This wisdom without understanding
Is of so absolute a force
No wise man of whatever standing
Can ever stand against its course,
Unless they tap its wondrous source,
To know so much, though knowing naught,
They pass all knowledge with their thought.

This summit all so steeply towers
And is of excellence so high
No human faculties or powers
Can ever to the top come nigh.
Whoever with its steep could vie,
Though knowing nothing, would transcend
All thought, forever, without end.

If you would ask, what is its essence—
This summit of all sense and knowing:
It comes from the Divinest Presence—
The sudden sense of Him outflowing,
In His great clemency bestowing
The gift that leaves men knowing naught,
Yet passing knowledge with their thought.

V

Coplas del alma que pena por ver a Dios, del mismo auctor

Vivo sin vivir en mí,
Y de tal manera espero,
Que muero porque no muero.

En mí yo no vivo ya,
Y sin Dios vivir no puedo;
Pues sin él y sin mí quedo,
Este vivir ¿qué será?
Mil muertes se me hará,
Pues mi misma vida espero,
Muriendo porque no muero.

Esta vida que yo vivo
Es privación de vivir;
Y así, es contino morir
Hasta que viva contigo.
Oye, mi Dios, lo que digo,
Que esta vida no la quiero;
Que muero porque no muero.

Estando absente de ti,
¿Qué vida puedo tener,
Sino muerte padescer,
La mayor que nunca vi?
Lástima tengo de mí,
Pues de suerte persevero,
Que muero porque no muero.

El pez que del agua sale,
Aun de alivio no caresce,

V

Coplas about the soul which suffers with impatience to see God

I live without inhabiting
Myself—in such a wise that I
Am dying that I do not die.

Within myself I do not dwell
Since without God I cannot live.
Reft of myself, and God as well,
What serves this life (I cannot tell)
Except a thousand deaths to give?
Since waiting here for life I lie
And die because I do not die.

This life I live in vital strength
Is loss of life unless I win You:
And thus to die I shall continue
Until in You I live at length.
Listen (my God!) my life is in You.
This life I do not want, for I
Am dying that I do not die.

Thus in your absence and your lack
How can I in myself abide
Nor suffer here a death more black
Than ever was by mortal died.
For pity of myself I've cried
Because in such a plight I lie
Dying because I do not die.

The fish that from the stream is lost
Derives some sort of consolation

Que en la muerte que padesce,
Al fin la muerte le vale.
¿Qué muerte habrá que se iguale
A mi vivir lastimero,
Pues si más vivo más muero?

Cuando me pienso aliviar
De verte en el Sacramento,
Háceme más sentimiento
El no te poder gozar;
Todo es para más penar,
Por no verte como quiero,
Y muero porque no muero.

Y si me gozo, Señor,
Con esperanza de verte,
En ver que puedo perderte
Se me dobla mi dolor:
Viviendo en tanto pavor,
Y esperando como espero,
Muérome porque no muero.

Sácame de aquesta muerte,
Mi Dios, y dame la vida;
No me tengas impedida
En este lazo tan fuerte;
Mira que peno por verte,
Y mi mal es tan entero,
Que muero porque no muero.

Lloraré mi muerte ya,
Y lamentaré mi vida
En tanto que detenida
Por mis pecados está.
¡Oh mi Dios! ¿cuándo será?
Cuando yo diga de vero:
Vivo ya porque no muero.

That in his death he pays the cost
At least of death's annihilation.
To this dread life with which I'm crossed
What fell death can compare, since I,
The more I live, the more must die.

When thinking to relieve my pain
I in the sacraments behold You
It brings me greater grief again
That to myself I cannot fold You.
And that I cannot see you plain
Augments my sorrow, so that I
Am dying that I do not die.

If in the hope I should delight,
Oh Lord, of seeing You appear,
The thought that I might lose Your sight
Doubles my sorrow and my fear.
Living as I do in such fright,
And yearning as I yearn, poor I
Must die because I do not die.

Oh rescue me from such a death
My God, and give me life, not fear;
Nor keep me bound and struggling here
Within the bonds of living breath.
Look how I long to see You near,
And how in such a plight I lie
Dying because I do not die!

I shall lament my death betimes,
And mourn my life, that it must be
Kept prisoner by sins and crimes
So long before I am set free:
Ah God, my God, when shall it be?
When I may say (and tell no lie)
I live because I've ceased to die?

V I

Otras del mismo a lo divino

Tras de un amoroso lance,
Y no de esperanza falto,
Volé tan alto, tan alto,
Que le dí a la caza alcance.

Para que yo alcance diese
A aqueste lance divino,
Tanto volar me convino,
Que de vista me perdiese;
Y con todo, en este trance
En el vuelo quedé falto;
Mas el amor fué tan alto,
Que le dí a la caza alcance.

Cuando más alto subía,
Deslumbróseme la vista,
Y la más fuerte conquista
En escuro se hacía;
Mas por ser de amor el lance
Dí un ciego y oscuro salto,
Y fuí tan alto, tan alto,
Que le dí a la caza alcance.

Cuanto más alto llegaba
De este lance tan subido,
Tanto más bajo y rendido
Y abatido me hallaba.
Dije: No habrá quien alcance;
Y abatíme tanto, tanto,
Que fuí tan alto, tan alto,
Que le dí a la caza alcance.

VI

Other verses with a divine meaning by the same author

Not without hope did I ascend
Upon an amorous quest to fly
And up I soared so high, so high,
I seized my quarry in the end.

As on this falcon quest I flew
To chase a quarry so divine,
I had to soar so high and fine
That soon I lost myself from view.
With loss of strength my plight was sorry
From straining on so steep a course.
But love sustained me with such force
That in the end I seized my quarry.

The more I rose into the height
More dazzled, blind, and lost I spun.
The greatest conquest ever won
I won in blindness, like the night.
Because love urged me on my way
I gave that mad, blind, reckless leap
That soared me up so high and steep
That in the end I seized my prey.

The steeper upward that I flew
On so vertiginous a quest
The humbler and more lowly grew
My spirit, fainting in my breast.
I said 'None yet can find the way'
But as my spirit bowed more low,
Higher and higher did I go
Till in the end I seized my prey.

Por una extraña manera
Mil vuelos pasé de un vuelo,
Porque esperanza de cielo
Tanto alcanza cuanto espera;
Esperé sólo este lance,
Y en esperar no fuí falto,
Pues fuí tan alto, tan alto,
Que le dí a la caza alcance.

By such strange means did I sustain
A thousand starry flights in one,
Since hope of Heaven yet by none
Was ever truly hoped in vain.
Only by hope I won my way
Nor did my hope my aim belie,
Since I soared up so high, so high,
That in the end I seized my prey.

VII

Otras canciones a lo divino (del mismo autor) de Cristo y el alma

Un pastorcico solo está penado,
Ajeno de placer y de contento,
Y en su pastora puesto el pensamiento,
Y el pecho del amor muy lastimado.

No llora por haberle amor llagado,
Que no le pena verse así afligido,
Aunque en el corazón está herido;
Mas llora por pensar que está olvidado.

Que sólo de pensar que está olvidado
De su bella pastora, con gran pena
Se deja, maltratar en tierra ajena,
El pecho del amor muy lastimado.

Y dice el Pastorcico: ¡Ay, desdichado
De aquel que de mi amor ha hecho ausencia,
Y no quiere gozar la mi presencia,
Y el pecho por su amor muy lastimado!

Y a cabo de un gran rato se ha encumbrado
Sobre un árbol do abrió sus brazos bellos,
Y muerto se ha quedado, asido de ellos,
El pecho del amor muy lastimado.

VII

Other songs concerning Christ and the soul

A shepherd lad was mourning his distress,
Far from all comfort, friendless and forlorn.
He fixed his thought upon his shepherdess
Because his breast by love was sorely torn.

He did not weep that love had pierced him so,
Nor with self-pity that the shaft was shot,
Though deep into his heart had sunk the blow,
It grieved him more that he had been forgot.

Only to think that he had been forgotten
By his sweet shepherdess, with travail sore,
He let his foes (in foreign lands begotten)
Gash the poor breast that love had gashed before.

'Alas! Alas! for him', the Shepherd cries,
'Who tries from me my dearest love to part
So that she does not gaze into my eyes
Or see that I am wounded to the heart.'

Then, after a long time, a tree he scaled,
Opened his strong arms bravely wide apart,
And clung upon that tree till death prevailed,
So sorely was he wounded in his heart.

VIII

Cantar del alma que se huelga de conoscer a Dios por fe

Que bien sé yo la fonte que mana y corre,
Aunque es de noche.

Aquella eterna fonte está ascondida,
Que bien sé yo do tiene su manida,
Aunque es de noche.

Su origen no lo sé, pues no le tiene,
Mas sé que todo origen de ella viene,
Aunque es de noche.

Sé que no puede ser cosa tan bella,
Y que cielos y tierra beben de ella,
Aunque es de noche.

Bien sé que suelo en ella no se halla,
Y que ninguno puede vadealla,
Aunque es de noche.

Su claridad nunca es escurecida,
Y sé que toda luz de ella es venida,
Aunque es de noche.

Sé ser tan caudalosas sus corrientes,
Que infiernos, cielos riegan, y las gentes,
Aunque es de noche.

El corriente que nace de esta fuente,
Bien sé que es tan capaz y omnipotente,
Aunque es de noche.

VIII

Song of the soul that is glad to know God by faith

How well I know that fountain's rushing flow
Although by night

Its deathless spring is hidden. Even so
Full well I guess from whence its sources flow
Though it be night.

Its origin (since it has none) none knows:
But that all origin from it arose
Although by night.

I know there is no other thing so fair
And earth and heaven drink refreshment there
Although by night.

Full well I know its depth no man can sound
And that no ford to cross it can be found
Though it be night.

Its clarity unclouded still shall be:
Out of it comes the light by which we see
Though it be night.

Flush with its banks the stream so proudly swells;
I know it waters nations, heavens, and hells
Though it be night.

The current that is nourished by this source
I know to be omnipotent in force
Although by night.

El corriente que de estas dos procede
Sé que ninguna de ellas le precede,
Aunque es de noche.

Aquesta eterna fonte está escondida
En este vivo pan por darnos vida,
Aunque es de noche.

Aquí se está llamando a las criaturas,
Y de esta agua se hartan, aunque a escuras,
Porque es de noche.

Aquesta viva fuente, que deseo,
En este pan de vida yo la veo,
Aunque de noche.

From source and current a new current swells
Which neither of the other twain excels
Though it be night.

The eternal source hides in the Living Bread
That we with life eternal may be fed
Though it be night.

Here to all creatures it is crying, hark!
That they should drink their fill though in the dark,
For it is night.

This living fount which is to me so dear
Within the bread of life I see it clear
Though it be night.

IX

Sobre el Evangelio 'In principio erat Verbum' acerca de la Santísima Trinidad

En el principio moraba
El Verbo, y en Dios vivía,
En quien su felicidad
Infinita poseía.

El mismo Verbo Dios era,
Que el principio se decía;
Él moraba en el principio,
Y principio no tenía.

Él era el mismo principio;
Por eso de él carecía;
El Verbo se llama Hijo
Que del principio nacía.

Hale siempre concebido,
Y siempre le concebía,
Dale siempre su sustancia,
Y siempre se la tenía.

Y así, la gloria del Hijo
Es la que en el Padre había,
Y toda su gloria el Padre
En el Hijo poseía.

Como amado en el amante
Uno en otro residía,
Y aquese amor que los une,
En lo mismo convenía,

[48]

IX

Upon the Gospel 'In the Beginning was the Word' relating to the Most Holy Trinity

In the beginning of all things
The Word lived in the Lord at rest.
And His felicity in Him
Was from infinity possessed.

That very Word was God Himself
By which all being was begun
For He lived in the beginning
And beginning had He none.

He Himself was the beginning,
So He had none, being one.
What was born of the beginning
Was the Word we call the Son.

Even so has God conceived Him
And conceived Him always so,
Ever giving Him the substance
As He gave it long ago.

And thus the glory of the Son
Is the glory of the Sire
And the glory of the Father
From His Son He does acquire.

As the loved-one in the lover
Each in the other's heart resided:
And the love that makes them one
Into one of them divided,

Con el uno y con el otro
En igualdad y valía:
Tres Personas y un amado
Entre todos tres había.

Y un amor en todas ellas
Y un amante las hacía;
Y el amante es el amado
En que cada cual vivía;

Que el ser que los tres poseen,
Cada cual le poseía,
Y cada cual de ellos ama
A la que este ser tenía.

Este ser es cada una,
Y éste sólo las unía
En un inefable nudo
Que decir no se sabía

Por lo cual era infinito
El amor que las unía,
Porque un solo amor tres tienen,
Que su esencia se decía;
Que el amor, cuanto más uno,
Tanto más amor hacía.

Then with one and with the other
Mated in such equality,
Three Persons now and one Beloved
They numbered, though they still were three.

There is one love in all three Persons:
One lover all the Three provides;
And the beloved is the lover
Which in each of them resides.

The Being which all three possess
Each of them does possess alone:
And each of them loves what that Being
Itself possesses of its own.

This very Being is Each One,
And it alone, in its own way,
Has bound them in that wondrous knot
Whose mystery no man can say.

Thus lives undying and eternal
The love that has entwined them so,
Because one love the three united
Which as their Essence now we know,
And this one love, the more in one-ness,
The more and more in love will grow.

X

ROMANCE II

De la comunicación de las tres Personas

En aquel amor inmenso
Que de los dos procedía,
Palabras de gran regalo
El Padre al Hijo decía,

De tan profundo deleite,
Que nadie las entendía;
Sólo el Hijo lo gozaba,
Que es a quien pertenecía.

Pero aquello que se entiende
De esta manera decía:
Nada me contenta, Hijo,
Fuera de tu compañía.

Y si algo me contenta,
En ti mismo lo quería;
El que a ti más se parece,
A mí más satisfacía.

Y el que nada te semeja,
En mí nada hallaría;
En ti sólo me he agradado,
¡Oh vida de vida mía!

X

ROMANCE II

Of the communion of the three Persons

Out of the love immense and bright
That from the two had thus begun,
Words of ineffable delight
The Father spoke unto the Son:

Words of so infinite a rapture
Their drift by none could be explained:
Only the Son their sense could capture
That only to Himself pertained.

What of them we can sense the clearest
Was in this manner said and thought:
Out of Your company, my Dearest,
I can be satisfied by nought.

But if aught please me, I as duly
In You, Yourself, the cause construe.
The one who satisfies Me truly
Is him who most resembles You.

He who in naught resembles You
Shall find of Me no trace or sign,
Life of My Life! for only through
Your own can I rejoice in Mine.

Eres lumbre de mi lumbre,
Eres mi sabiduría,
Figura de mi sustancia,
En quien bien me complacía.

Al que a ti te amare, Hijo,
A mí mismo le daría,
Y el amor yo en ti tengo,
Ese mismo en él pondría,
En razón de haber amado
A quien yo tanto quería.

You are the brilliance of My light
My wisdom and My power divine,
The figure of My substance bright
In whom I am well pleased to shine!

The man who loves You, O my Son,
To him Myself I will belong.
The love that in Yourself I won
I'll plant in him and root it strong,
Because he loved the very one
I loved so deeply and so long.

XI

ROMANCE III

De la Creación

Una esposa que te ame,
Mi Hijo, darte quería,
Que por tu valor merezca
Tener nuestra compañía.

Y comer pan a una mesa,
Del mismo que yo comía;
Porque conozca los bienes
Que en tal Hijo yo tenía.
Y se congracie conmigo
De tu gracia y lozanía.

Mucho lo agradezco, Padre,
El Hijo le respondía;
A la esposa que me dieres,
Yo mi claridad daría,

Para que por ella vea
Cuánto mi Padre valía,
Y cómo el ser que poseo,
De su ser le recibía.

Reclinarla he yo en mi brazo
Y en tu amor se abrasaría,
Y con eterno deleite
Tu bondad sublimaría.

XI

ROMANCE III

Of the Creation

I wish to give You, My dear Son,
To cherish You, a lovely bride,
And one who for Your worth will merit
To live forever by Our side.

And she will eat bread at our table
The selfsame bread on which I've fed:
That she may know the worth and value
Of the Son whom I have bred,
And there enjoy with Me forever
The grace and glory that You shed.

'Thanks to You, Almighty Father,'
The Son made answer to the Sire,
'To the wife that You shall give Me
I shall give My lustrous fire,

'That by its brightness she may witness
How infinite My Father's worth
And how My being from Your being
In every way derived its birth.

'I'll hold her on My arm reclining
And with Your love will burn her so
That with an endless joy and wonder
Your loving kindness she may know.'

XII

ROMANCE IV

Hágase, pues, dijo el Padre,
Que tu amor lo merecía:
Y en este dicho que dijo,
El mundo criado había.

Palacio para la esposa,
Hecho en gran sabiduría;
El cual, en dos aposentos,
Alto y bajo, dividía.

El bajo de diferencias
Infinitas componía;
Mas el alto hermoseaba
De admirable pedrería.

Porque conozca la esposa
El Esposo que tenía,
En el alto colocaba
La angélica jerarquía;

Pero la natura humana
En el bajo la ponía,
Por ser en su compostura
Algo de menor valía.

Y aunque el ser y los lugares
De esta suerte los partía,
Pero todos son un cuerpo
De la esposa que decía:

[58]

XII

ROMANCE IV

'Let it be done, then,' said the Father,
'For Your love's surpassing worth.'
And the moment he pronounced it
Was the creation of the Earth.

For the bride He built a palace
Out of His knowledge vast and grand,
Which in two separate compartments,
One high, one low, He wisely planned.

The lower storey was of endless
Differences composed: the higher
He beautified with wondrous jewels,
Refulgent with supernal fire.

That the bride might know her Bridegroom
In the true glory of His power,
In the top part He set the angels
In shining hierarchy to tower.

But, tenant of the lower mansion
Our human nature was assigned
Because its human composition
Falls short of the angelic kind.

And though the Being in two places
He divided in this way,
He composed of both one body
To house the Bride, who thus did say:

Que el amor de un mismo Esposo
Una Esposa los hacía:
Los de arriba poseían
El Esposo en alegría;

Los de abajo en esperanza
De fe que les infundía,
Diciéndoles que algún tiempo
Él los engrandecería.

Y que aquella su bajeza
Él se la levantaría,
De manera que ninguno
Ya la vituperaría.

Porque en todo semejante
Él a ellos se haría,
Y se vendría con ellos,
Y con ellos moraría.

Y que Dios sería hombre,
Y que el hombre Dios sería,
Y trataría con ellos,
Comería y bebería.

Y que con ellos continuo
Él mismo se quedaría,
Hasta que se consumase
Este siglo que corría.

Cuando se gozaran juntos
En eterna melodía;
Porque él era la cabeza
De la esposa que tenía.

[60]

That the love of one sole Bridegroom
Made them into one sole Bride.
Those of the upper part possessed Him
In deathless joy beatified:

Those underneath, in hope and yearning,
Born of the faith He brings to birth,
By telling them that surely, sometime,
His love will magnify their worth;

And all in them that's base and lowly
He would exalt to such degree
That none who after that beheld it
Would scorn its first humility.

Exactly, in all things like they are,
He would cause Himself to be.
He would traffic in their dealings
And in their daily life agree.

And so the God would be the Man
And the Man be the God: and then
He would roam amongst them freely
And eat and drink with other men.

He will stay with us forever.
As a Comrade He will stay,
Till the present dispensation
Is consumed and fades away.

Then, to a deathless music sounding,
Bride to Bridegroom will be pressed,
Because He is the crown and headpiece
Of the Bride that He possessed.

[61]

A la cual todos los miembros
De los justos juntaría,
Que son cuerpo de la esposa,
A la cual él tomaría.

En sus brazos tiernamente,
Y allí su amor la daría;
Y que así juntos en uno
Al Padre la llevaría.

Donde del mismo deleite
Que Dios goza, gozaría;
Que, como el Padre y el Hijo,
Y el que de ellos procedía,

El uno vive en el otro;
Así la esposa sería,
Que, dentro de Dios absorta,
Vida de Dios viviría.

To her beauty all the members
Of the just He will enlace
To form the body of the Bride
When taken into His embrace.

Tenderly in His arms He'll take her
With all the force that God can give
And draw her nearer to the Father
All in one unison to live.

There with the single, same rejoicing
With which God revels, she will thrill,
Revelling with the Son, the Father,
And that which issues from Their will,

Each one living in the other;
Samely loved, clothed, fed, and shod.
She, absorbed in Him forever,
She will live the Life of God.

XIII

ROMANCE V

Con esta buena esperanza
Que de arriba les venía,
El tedio de sus trabajos
Más leve se les hacía;

Pero la esperanza larga
Y el deseo que crecía
De gozarse con su Esposo
Continuo les afligía.

Por lo cual con oraciones,
Con suspiros y agonía,
Con lágrimas y gemidos
Le rogaban noche y día

Que ya se determinase
A les dar su compañía.
Unos decían: ¡Oh, si fuese
En mi tiempo el alegría!

Otros: Acaba, Señor;
Al que has de enviar envía.
Otros: Oh si ya rompieses
Esos cielos, y vería

Con mis ojos, que bajases,
Y mi llanto cesaría;
Regad, nubes de lo alto,
Que la tierra lo pedía,

Y ábrase ya la tierra,
Que espinas nos producía,
Y produzca aquella flor
Con que ella florecería.

XIII

ROMANCE V

With the blest hope of this union
Coming to them from on high,
All the tedium of their labour
Seemed to glide more lightly by.

But the length of endless waiting
And the increase of desire
To enjoy the blessed Bridegroom
Was to them affliction dire.

So they made continual prayer
With sighs of piteous dismay,
And with groans and lamentations
Pleaded with Him night and day

That He would decide with them
To share His company at last.
'Oh if but this thing could happen,'
They cried, 'before our time be past.'

Others cried: 'Come Lord and end it!
Him You have promised, send Him now!'
Others: 'If only You would sunder
Those skies, and to my sight allow

'The vision of Yourself descending
To make my lamentations cease;
Cloud in the height, rain down upon us
That the earth may find release.

'Let the earth be cleft wide open
That bore us thorns so sharp and sour
And now at last produce the Blossom
With which it was ordained to flower.'

Otros decían: ¡Oh dichoso
El que en tal tiempo sería,
Que merezca ver a Dios
Con los ojos que tenía,

Y tratarle con sus manos,
Y andar en su compañía,
Y gozar de los misterios
Que entonces ordenaría!

Others said: 'Oh happy people
Who will be living in those years
And will deserve to see the Bridegroom
With their own eyes when He appears:,

'Who with their own hands then will touch Him,
And walk in friendship by His side,
And there enjoy the sacred mysteries,
That in His reign He will provide.'

XIV

ROMANCE VI

En aquestos y otros ruegos
Gran tiempo pasado había;
Pero en los postreros años
El fervor mucho crecía.

Cuando el viejo Simeón
En deseo se encendía,
Rogando a Dios que quisiese
Dejalle ver este día.

Y así, el Espíritu Santo
Al buen viejo respondía
Que le daba su palabra
Que la muerte no vería

Hasta que la vida viese,
Que de arriba decendía,
Y que él en sus mismas manos
Al mismo Dios tomaría,
Y le tendría en sus brazos,
Y consigo abrazaría.

XIV

ROMANCE VI

In these and other supplications
A long age went slowly past,
But in later times the longing
Grew so fervent that, at last,

The aged Simeon, taking fire
With inward love, knelt down to pray,
Beseeching God that He would grant him
He might be spared to see the day.

And the Holy Spirit answering
To his pleadings made reply
Giving him His word that truly
He would never come to die

Till from on high he should behold
The Light descending on its quest,
Till he took in his own hands
God Himself, to be caressed,
Folded his arms about Him fondly
And held Him closely to his breast

XV

ROMANCE VII

Prosigue la Encarnación

Ya que el tiempo era llegado
En que hacerse convenía
El rescate de la esposa
Que en duro yugo servía,

Debajo de aquella ley
Que Moisés dado le había,
El Padre con amor tierno
De esta manera decía:

Ya ves, Hijo, que a tu esposa
A tu imagen hecho había,
Y en lo que a ti se parece
Contigo bien convenía;

Pero difiere en la carne,
Que en tu simple ser no había;
En los amores perfectos
Esta ley se requería,

Que se haga semejante
El amante a quien quería,
Que la mayor semejanza
Más deleite contenía.

El cual sin duda en tu esposa
Grandemente crecería
Si te viere semejante
En la carne que tenía.

XV

ROMANCE VII

Continues the Incarnation

Now that the time was truly come
The ancient order to revoke
And pay the ransom of the bride
Serving in so hard a yoke,

Under that former law which Moses
Of old upon her shoulders laid—
The Father, in His love most tender,
To the Son, His thought displayed:

'You see how Your beloved bride
After Your image has been made.
In what she most resembles You
Her loveliness I have arrayed,

'Though differing from You by that flesh
Your finer nature never knew;
There is in every perfect love
A law to be accomplished too:

'That the lover should resemble
The belov'd: and be the same.
And the greater is the likeness
Brighter will the rapture flame.

'That which to Your own beloved
Greater rapture would provide
Would be to behold that likeness
In the flesh with her allied.'

Mi voluntad es la tuya,
El Hijo le respondía,
Y la gloria que yo tengo,
Es tu voluntad ser mía.

Y a mí me conviene, Padre,
Lo que tu Alteza decía,
Porque por esta manera
Tu bondad más se vería.

Veráse tu gran potencia,
Justicia y sabiduría,
Irélo a decir al mundo,
Y noticia le daría
De tu belleza y dulzura
Y de tu soberanía.

Iré a buscar a mi esposa,
Y sobre mí tomaría
Sus fatigas y trabajos,
En que tanto padescía.

Y porque ella vida tenga,
Y por ella moriría,
Y sacándola del lago,
A ti te la volvería.

The Son then answered to the Father,
'My will is Yours and Yours alone,
And the glory that I shine with
Is My will to work Your own.

'That which Your Grace says, O My Father,
In everything appears the best
Since most clearly in this manner
Can Your kindness be professed.

'Thus Your omnipotence, and justice,
And wisdom will be well descried,
I will tell it to the world,
And spread the tidings far and wide
Of Your beauty, power, and sweetness
In one sovereignty allied.'

'I will go now and seek My bride,
And take upon My shoulders strong
The cares, the weariness, and labours
Which she has suffered for so long.

And that she may win new life
I myself for her will die,
Rescue her from the burning lake,
And bear her back to You on high.'

XVI

Prosigue

Entonces llamó un arcángel,
Que San Gabriel se decía,
Y enviólo a una doncella
Que se llamaba María,

De cuyo consentimiento
El misterio se hacía;
En la cual la Trinidad
De carne al Verbo vestía.

Y aunque tres hacen la obra,
En el uno se hacía;
Y quedó el Verbo encarnado
En el vientre de María.

Y el que tenía sólo Padre,
Ya también Madre tenía,
Aunque no como cualquiera
Que de varón concebía;

Que de las entrañas de ella
Él su carne recibía:
Por lo cual Hijo de Dios
Y del hombre se decía.

XVI

The same

Then He summoned an archangel,
Saint Gabriel: and when he came,
Sent him forth to find a maiden,
    Mary was her name.

Only through her consenting love
Could the mystery be preferred
That the Trinity in human
    Flesh might clothe the Word.

Though the three Persons worked the wonder
It only happened in the One.
So was the Word made incarnation
    In Mary's womb, a son.

So He who only had a Father
Now had a Mother undefiled,
Though not as ordinary maids
    Had she conceived the Child.

By Mary, and with her own flesh
He was clothed in His own frame:
Both Son of God and Son of Man
    Together had one name.

XVII

ROMANCE IX

Del Nacimiento

Ya que era llegado el tiempo
En que de nacer había,
Así como desposado
De su tálamo salía,

Abrazado con su esposa,
Que en sus brazos la traía,
Al cual la graciosa Madre
En un pesebre ponía,

Entre unos animales
Que a la sazón allí había:
Los hombres decían cantares,
Los ángeles melodía,

Festejando el desposorio
Que entre tales dos había;
Pero Dios en el pesebre
Allí lloraba y gemía,

Que eran joyas que la esposa
Al desposorio traía;
Y la Madre estaba en pasmo
De que tal trueque veía;

El llanto del hombre en Dios,
Y en el hombre la alegría,
Lo cual del uno y del otro
Tan ajeno ser solía.

XVII

ROMANCE IX

The Birth of Christ

Now that the season was approaching
Of His long-expected birth,
Like a bridegroom from his chamber
He emerged upon our earth

Clinging close to His beloved
Whom He brought along with Him.
While the gracious Mary placed them
In a manger damp and dim.

Amongst the animals that round it
At that season stretched their limbs,
Men were singing songs of gladness
And the angels chanting hymns,

To celebrate the wondrous marriage
By whose bond such two were tied,
But the wee God in the manger
He alone made moan and cried;

Tears were the jewels of the dowry
Which the bride with her had brought.
And the Mother gazed upon them
Nearly fainting at the thought.

The tears of Man in God alone,
The joy of God in men was seen.
Two things so alien to each other,
Or to the rule, had never been.

XVIII

Otro del mismo que va por 'Super flumina Babylonis'

Encima de las corrientes,
Que en Babilonia hallaba,
Allí me senté llorando,
Allí la tierra regaba.

Acordándome de ti,
Oh Sión, a quien amaba,
Era dulce tu memoria,
Y con ella más lloraba.

Dejé los trajes de fiesta,
Los de trabajo tomaba,
Y colgué en los verdes sauces
La música que llevaba.

Poniéndola en esperanza
De aquello que en ti esperaba;
Allí me hirió el amor,
Y el corazón me sacaba.

Díjele que me matase,
Pues de tal suerte llagaba:
Yo me metía en su fuego,
Sabiendo que me abrasaba,

Desculpando el avecica
Que en el fuego se acababa;
Estábame en mí muriendo,
Y en ti sólo respiraba.

En mí por ti me moría,
Y por ti resucitaba,
Que la memoria de ti
Daba vida y la quitaba.

[78]

XVIII

*A Poem by the same author which paraphrases
the Psalm, 'Super flumina Babylonis'*

Over the streams of running water
Which by Babylon are crowned,
There I sat, with bitter teardrops
Watering the alien ground.

I was full of your remembrance,
Sion, whom I loved of yore,
And the sweeter your remembrance
Bitterly I wept the more.

I cast off my costly garments,
Donned the working clothes you see,
And the harp that was my music
Hung upon a willow tree.

There to wait for the fulfilment
Of the hope I hoped in you.
There did love so sorely wound me
And my heart from me withdrew.

I entreated him to kill me
Since he'd wounded me so sore.
And I leaped into his fire
Knowing it would burn the more.

Now the fledgeling bird excusing
Who would perish in the fire,
In myself I may be dying,
Yet from you my life respire.

In myself for you I perished
Yet through you revive once more,
Whose remembrance gives me life
Which it took from me before.

Gozábanse los extraños
Entre quien cautivo estaba.
Preguntábanme cantares
De lo que en Sión cantaba;
Canta de Sión un himno,
Veamos cómo sonaba.

Decid: ¿Cómo en tierra ajena,
Donde por Sión lloraba,
Cantaré yo la alegría
Que en Sión se me quedaba?
Echaríala en olvido
Si en la ajena me gozaba.

Con mi paladar se junte
La lengua con que hablaba,
Si de ti yo me olvidare,
En la tierra do moraba.

Sión, por los verdes ramos
Que Babilonia me daba,
De mí se olvide mi diestra,
Que es lo que en ti más amaba,

Si de ti no me acordare,
En lo que más me gozaba,
Y si yo tuviere fiesta,
Y sin ti la festejaba.

¡Oh hija de Babilonia,
Mísera y desventurada!
Bienaventurado era
Aquel en quien confiaba,
Que te ha de dar el castigo
Que de tu mano llevaba.

Y juntará sus pequeños,
Y a mí, porque en ti lloraba,
A la piedra que era Cristo,
Por el cual yo te dejaba.

When the aliens were carousing
Where a captive I was found,
They would ask me for a ditty
From my Country's distant bound:
'Sing for us a hymn of Sion,
Let us hear how well they sound.'

How can I sing here in exile
Where I weep against my choice
For my Sion, and the raptures
Which in Sion thrilled my voice.
I would hurl her to oblivion
If abroad I could rejoice.

May it join unto my palate—
This same tongue with which I speak,
If to slight my native country
I should ever prove so weak!

Sion, by the deep green branches
Which in Babylon I see,
May my own right hand forget me
Which I loved the most when free,

If I let slip from my remembrance
What I most enjoyed in you,
Or I celebrate one feast-day
Save it be within your view.

Daughter of the Babylonians
Luckless and unhappy maid!
Bless'd and happy was the Person
Upon whom my trust was laid,
By whom the weary chastisement
Of your own hand will be repaid.

He will join me with his children,
Because to you my tears were due,
And bring me to the Rock of Jesus
By which I have escaped from you.

XIX

Glosa a lo divino

Sin arrimo y con arrimo,
Sin luz y a oscuras viviendo,
Todo me voy consumiendo.

Mi alma está desasida
De toda cosa criada,
Y sobre sí levantada,
Y en una sabrosa vida,
Sólo en su Dios arrimada.
Por eso ya se dirá
La cosa que más estimo,
Que mi alma se ve ya
Sin arrimo y con arrimo.

Y aunque tinieblas padezco
En esta vida mortal,
No es tan crecido mi mal;
Porque, si de luz carezco,
Tengo vida celestial;
Porque el amor de tal vida,
Cuando más ciego va siendo,
Que tiene al alma rendida,
Sin luz y a oscuras viviendo.

Hace tal obra el amor,
Después que le conocí,
Que, si hay bien o mal en mí,
Todo lo hace de un sabor,
Y al alma transforma en sí;
Y así, en su llama sabrosa,
La cual en mí estoy sintiendo,
Apriesa, sin quedar cosa,
Todo me voy consumiendo.

XIX

With a divine intention

Without support, yet well-supported,
Though in pitch-darkness, with no ray,
Entirely I am burned away.

My spirit is so freed from every
Created thing, that through the skies,
Above herself, she's lifted, flies,
And as in a most fragrant reverie,
Only on God her weight applies.
The thing which most my faith esteems
For this one fact will be reported—
Because my soul above me streams
Without support, yet well-supported.

What though I languish in the shades
As through my mortal life I go,
Not over-heavy is my woe
Since if no glow my gloom invades,
With a celestial life I glow.
The love of such a life, I say,
The more benightedly it darkens,
Turns more to that to which it hearkens,
Though in pitch-darkness, with no ray.

Since I knew Love, I have been taught
He can perform most wondrous labours.
Though good and bad in me are neighbours
He turns their difference to naught
Then both into Himself, so sweetly,
And with a flame so fine and fragrant
Which now I feel in me completely
Reduce my being, till no vagrant
Vestige of my own self can stay.
And wholly I am burned away.

XX

Glosa a lo divino del mismo autor

Por toda la hermosura
Nunca yo me perderé,
Si no por un no sé qué
Que se alcanza por ventura.

Sabor de bien que es finito,
Lo más que puede llegar,
Es cansar el apetito
Y estragar el paladar;
Y así, por toda dulzura
Nunca yo me perderé,
Sino por un no sé qué
Que se halla por ventura.

El corazón generoso
Nunca cura de parar
Donde se puede pasar,
Sino en más dificultoso;
Nada le causa hartura,
Y sube tanto su fe,
Que gusta de un no sé qué
Que se halla por ventura.

El que de amor adolece,
Del divino ser tocado,
Tiene el gusto tan trocado,
Que a los gustos desfallece;
Como el que con calentura
Fastidia el manjar que ve,
Y apetece un no sé qué
Que se halla por ventura.

[84]

XX

With a divine intention, by the same author

For all the beauty life has got
I'll never throw myself away
Save for one thing I know not what
Which lucky chance may bring my way.

The savour of all finite joy
In the long run amounts to this—
To tire the appetite of bliss
And the fine palate to destroy.
So for life's sweetness, all the lot,
I'll never throw myself away
But for a thing, I know not what,
Which lucky chance may bring my way.

The generous heart upon its quest
Will never falter, nor go slow,
But pushes on, and scorns to rest,
Wherever it's most hard to go.
It runs ahead and wearies not
But upward hurls its fierce advance
For it enjoys I know not what
That is achieved by lucky chance.

He that is growing to full growth
In the desire of God profound,
Will find his tastes so changed around
That of mere pleasures he is loth,
Like one who, with the fever hot,
At food will only look askance
But craves for that, he knows not what,
Which may be brought by lucky chance.

[85]

No os maravilléis de aquesto,
Que el gusto se quede tal,
Porque es la causa del mal
Ajena de todo el resto;
Y así, toda criatura
Enajenada se ve,
Y gusta de un no sé qué
Que se halla por ventura.

Que estando la voluntad
De Divinidad tocada,
No puede quedar pagada
Sino con Divinidad;
Mas, por ser tal su hermosura,
Que sólo se ve por fe,
Gústala en un no sé qué
Que se halla por ventura.

Pues de tal enamorado,
Decidme si habréis dolor,
Pues que no tiene sabor
Entre todo lo criado;
Sólo, sin forma y figura,
Sin hallar arrimo y pie,
Gustando allá un no sé qué
Que se halla por ventura.

No penséis que el interior,
Que es de mucha más valía,
Halla gozo y alegría
En lo que acá da sabor;
Mas sobre toda hermosura,
Y lo que es y será y fué,
Gusta de allá un no sé qué
Que se halla por ventura.

Do not amaze yourself at this
That pleasure is of earthly things
That cause from which most evil springs
And most the enemy of bliss.
And so all creatures earth-begot
Begin from it to turn their glance
And seek a thing, I know not what,
Which may be won by lucky chance.

For once the will has felt the hand
Of the Divine upon it set,
It never ceases to demand,
Divinity must pay the debt.
But since its loveliness to scan
Only true faith may steal a glance,
It finds it out as best it can
By risking on a lucky chance.

With love of One so high elated,
Tell me, if you would find great harm
If the servants He created
Did not rival Him in charm?
Alone, without face, form, or features,
Foothold, or prop, you would advance
To love that thing, beyond all creatures,
Which may be won by happy chance.

Think not that the interior sprite
Which is of vastly greater worth,
Can find among the joys of earth
Much for amusement or delight.
This world no beauty can advance
Which is, or ever was begot,
To vie with that, I know not what,
Which may be won by lucky chance.

Más emplea su cuidado
Quien se quiere aventajar,
En lo que está por ganar,
Que en lo que tiene ganado;
Y así, para más altura
Yo siempre me inclinaré
Sobre todo a un no sé qué
Que se halla por ventura.

Por lo que por el sentido
Puede acá comprehenderse,
Y todo lo que entenderse,
Aunque sea muy subido,
Ni por gracia y hermosura
Yo nunca me perderé,
Sino por un no sé qué
Que se halla por ventura.

XXI

Del Verbo divino

Del Verbo divino
La Virgen preñada
Viene de camino
Si le dais posada.

The man who strains for wealth and rank
Employs more care, and wastes more health
For riches that elude his stealth
Than those he's hoarded in the bank;
But I my fortune to advance
The lowlier stoop my lowly lot
Over some thing, I know not what,
Which may be found by lucky chance.

For that which by the sense down here
Is comprehended as our good,
And all that can be understood
Although it soars sublime and sheer;
For all that beauty can enhance—
I'll never lose my happy lot:
Only for that, I know not what,
Which can be won by lucky chance.

XXI

Concerning the Divine Word

With the divinest Word, the Virgin
Made pregnant, down the road
Comes walking, if you'll grant her
A room in your abode.

XXII

Suma de la perfección

Olvido de lo criado,
Memoria del Criador,
Atención a lo interior
Y estarse amando al Amado.

XXII

Summary of perfection

Ignoring the created and inferior;
Remembering above all things the Creator;
Attention to the life that is interior;
For the Beloved love that's always greater.